Party Legs

Susan Cunningham

ISBN: 978-0-9851902-5-5

Dedicated to my husband.

The adventure continues.

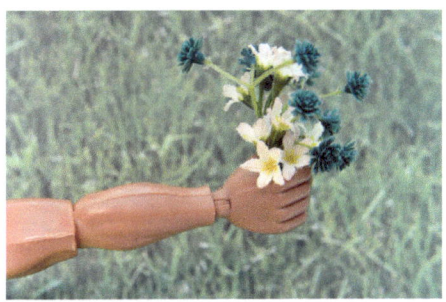

Forward

Every once in a while, I'll hear a giggle coming from the attic and know that Susan is up there playing with her community of dolls and toy animals, turning them into works of art.

Perhaps G.I. Joe is saving the world or making goo-goo eyes at Barbie, who just might be dancing at a party or lying on a pile of mattresses and somehow sensing that little pea buried at the bottom.

Or maybe bunnies are getting into all sorts of adorable trouble.

And then there's the one of gorillas scratching themselves and watching a football game on the toy TVs.

Hey wait, is this some sort of anti-Steve political statement? Am I - and all men - being photographically mocked and humiliated?

Ah, who cares … all that time Susan spends up in the attic playing with, posing and taking photos of her friends means more time for me to watch football.

And scratch myself.

Susan wanted to keep her toys in the attic photos to herself, but I convinced her that the world needs to know what I have to deal with on a day-to-day basis and all the crazy…

Wait, I mean: The world needs to see all the incredible creativity of Susan's parallel universe in our attic.

So go ahead, what are you waiting for, start turning the pages and looking at the photos. And, it's OK to giggle.

The artist's husband

January 2015

Atlas

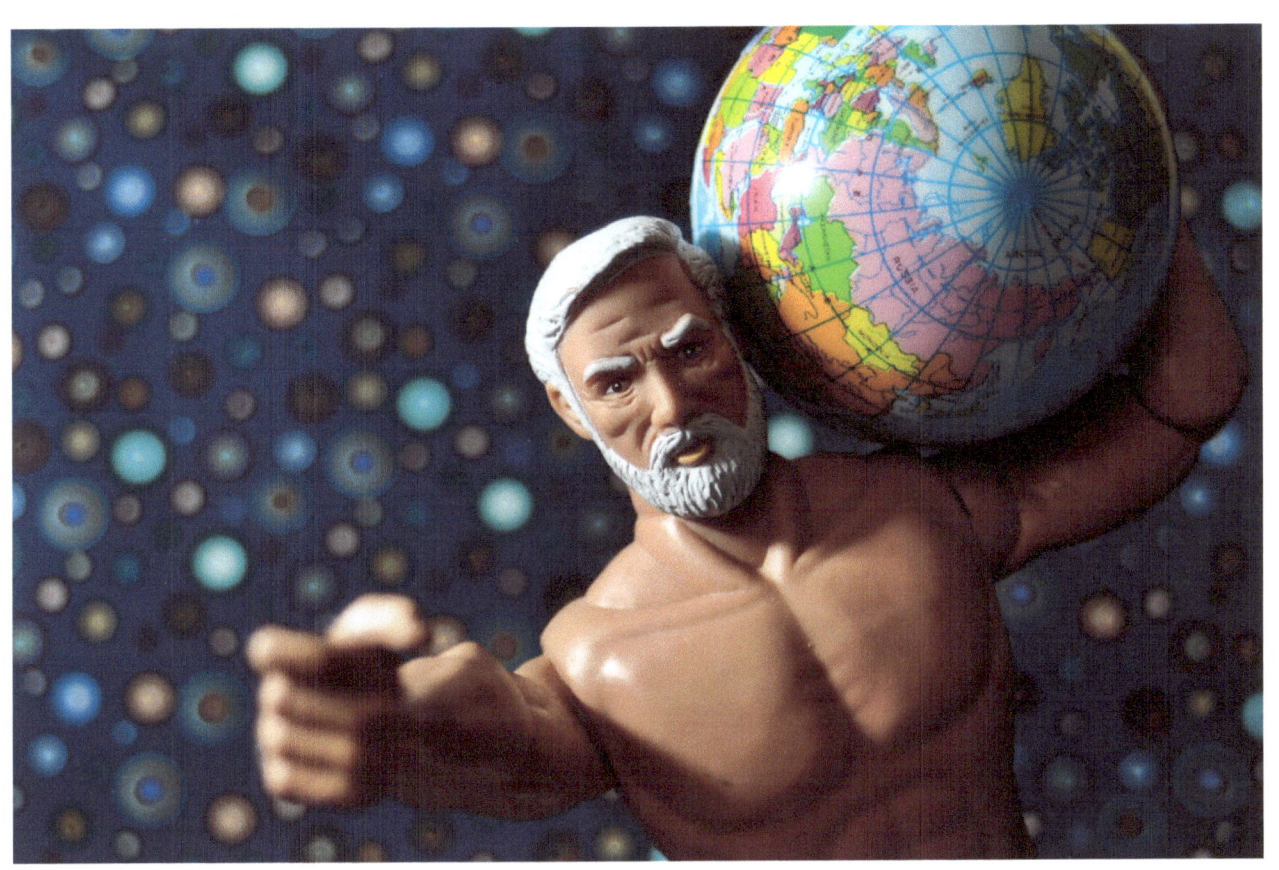

Surveillance

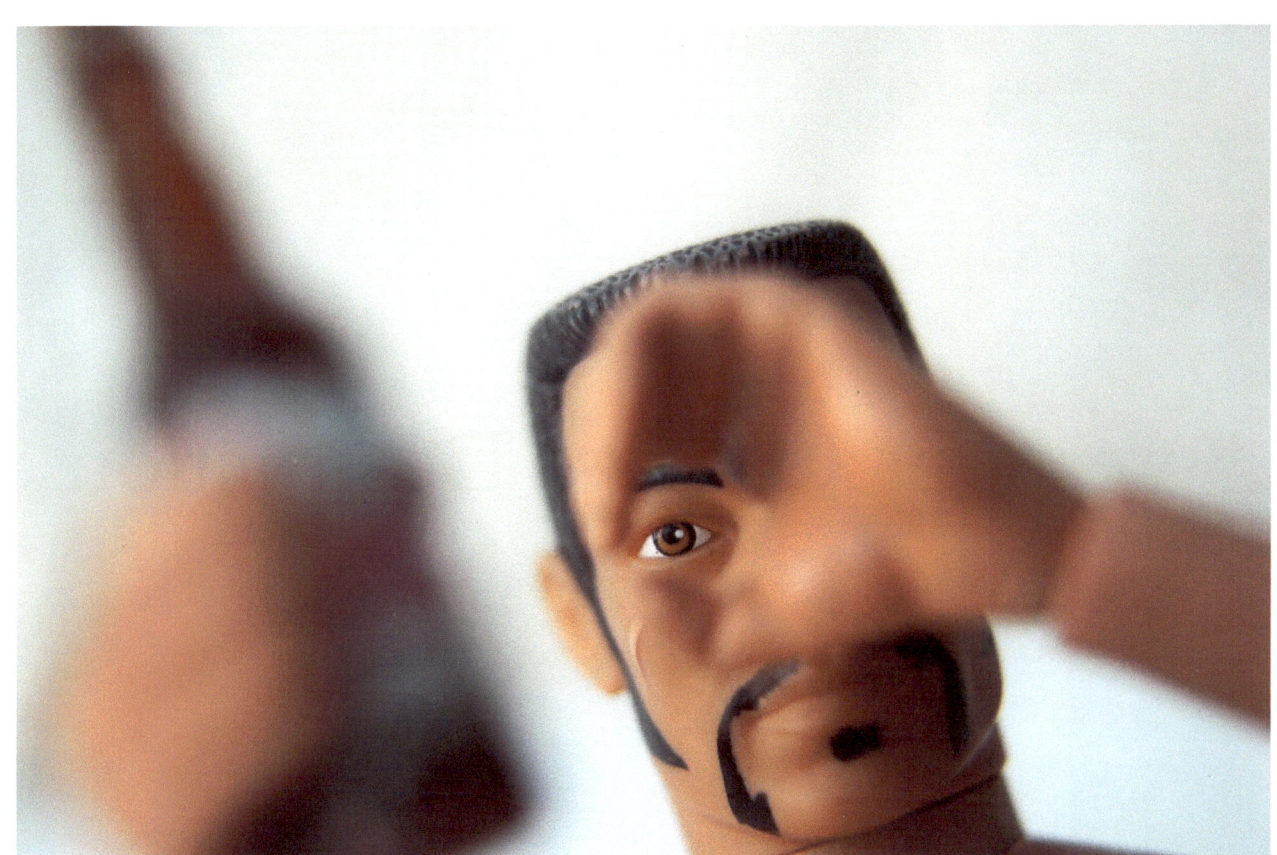

Weapons O' Mass Destruction

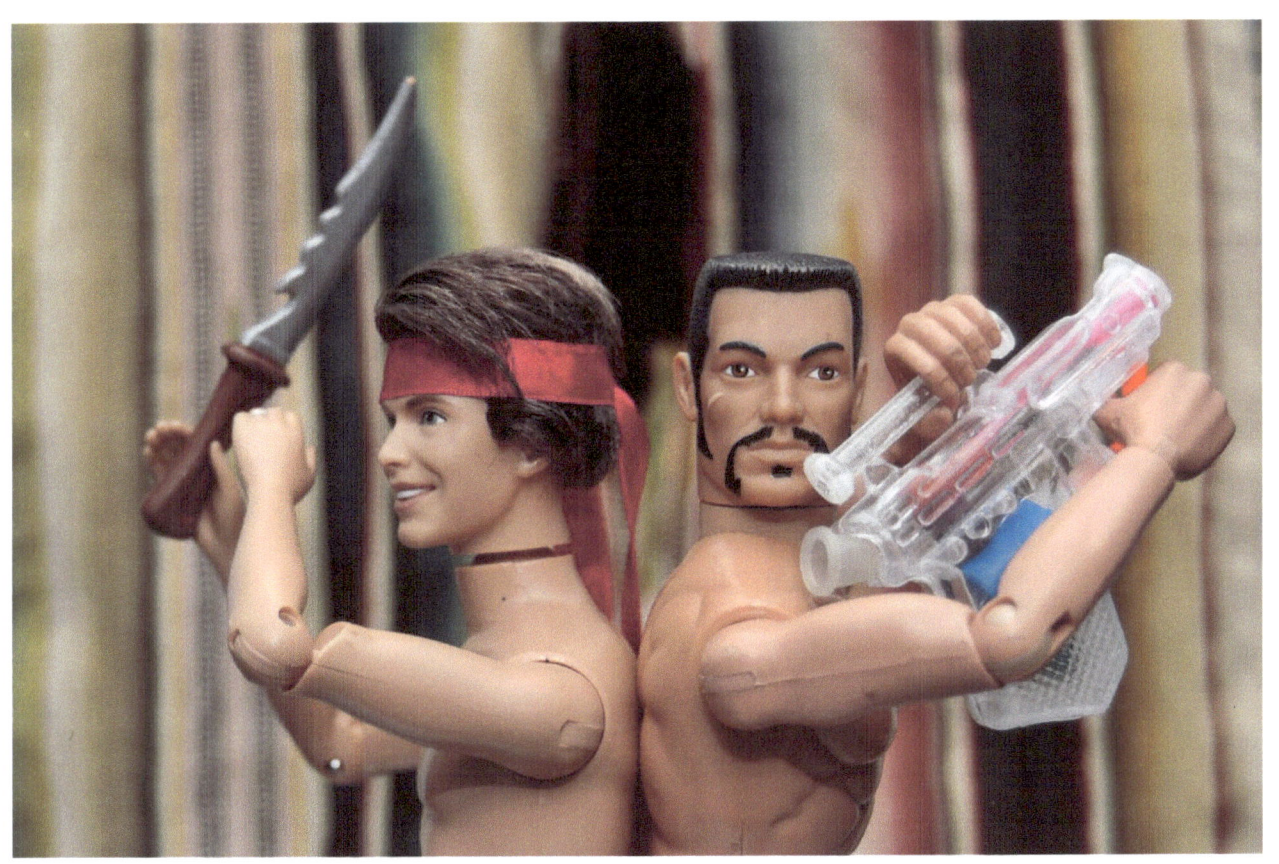

Joe & joe

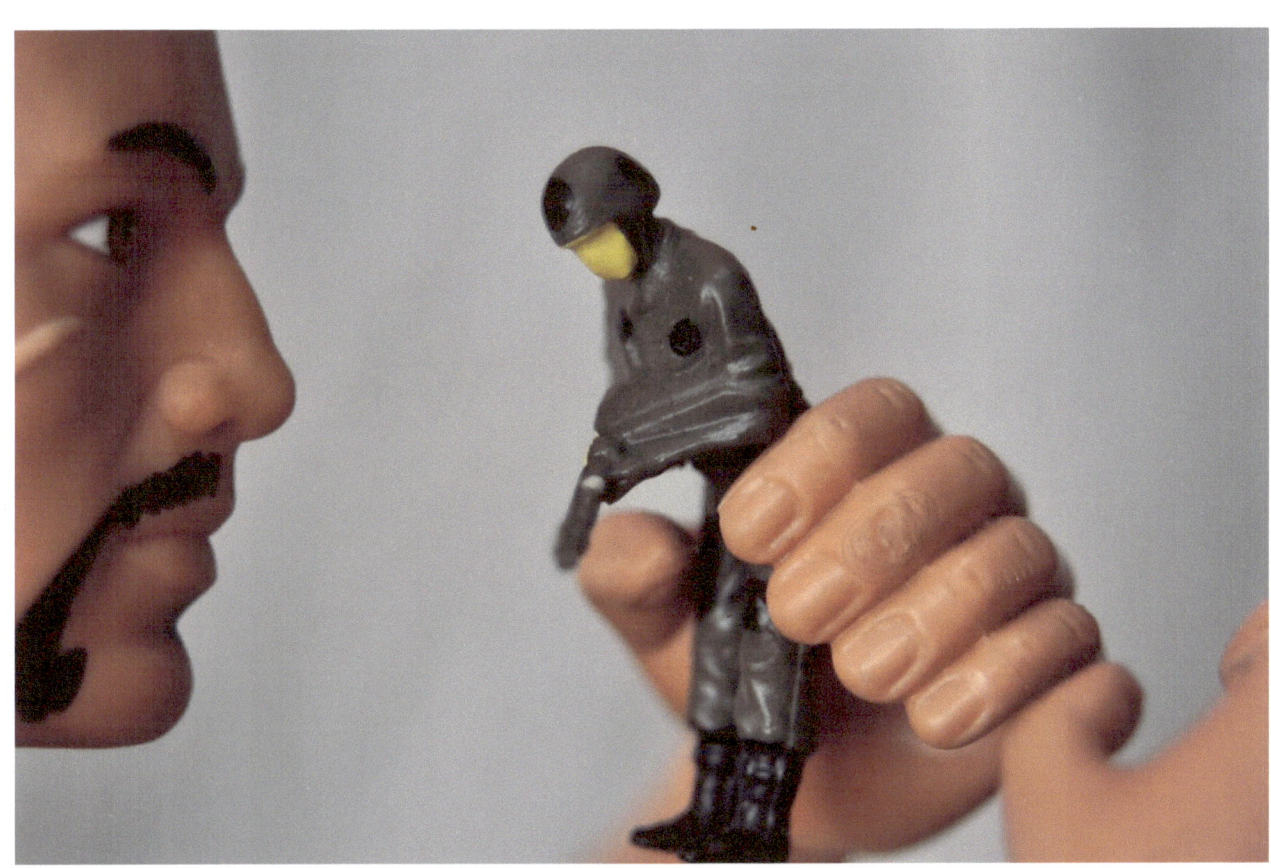

How the West Was Won

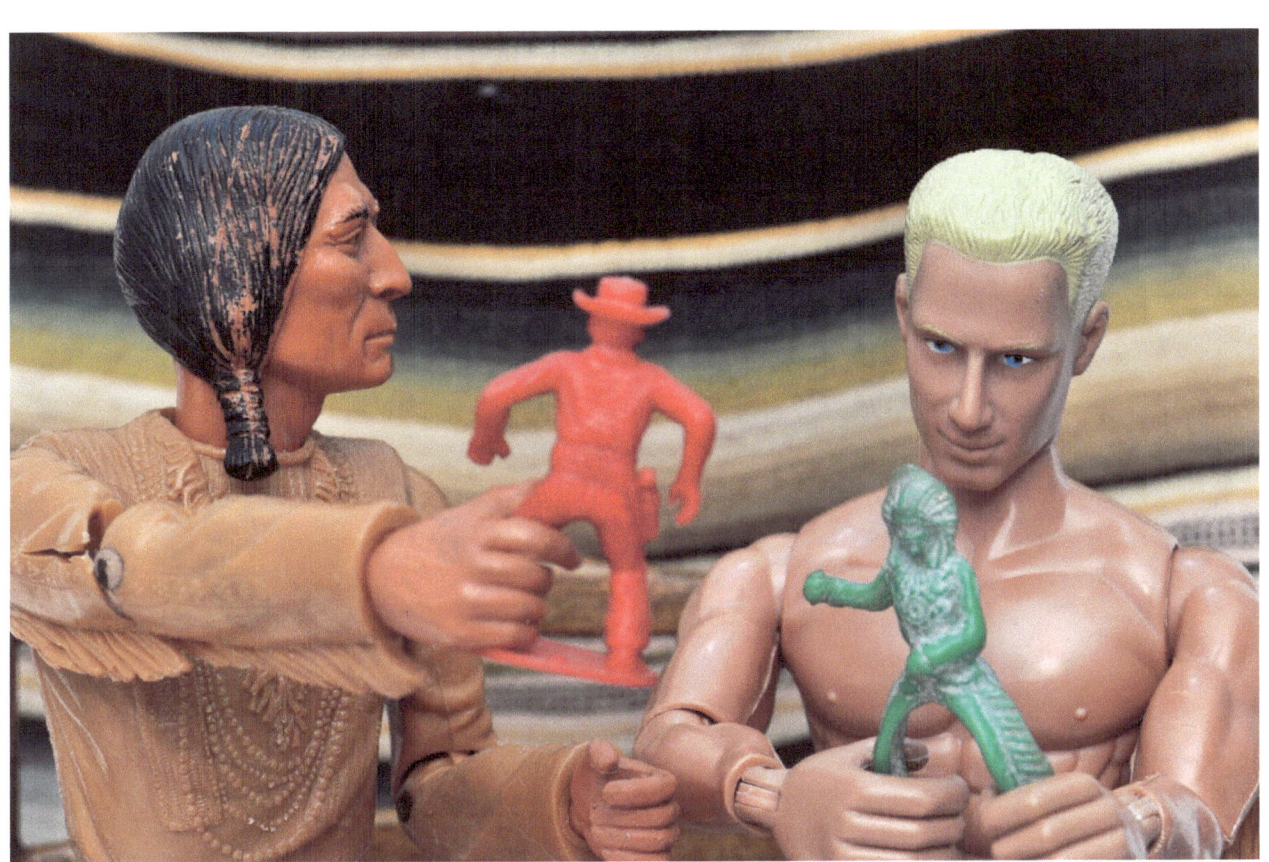

Party Legs

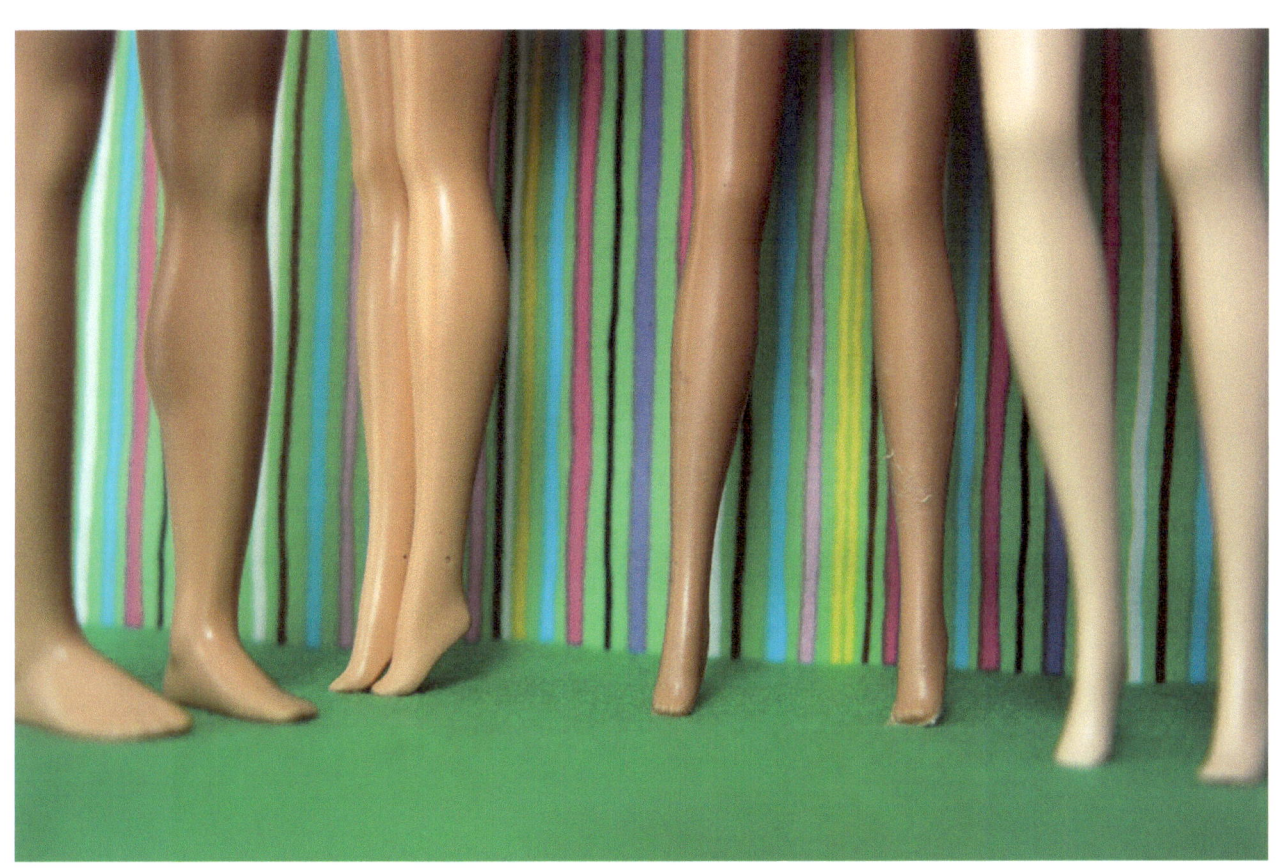

Party Arms

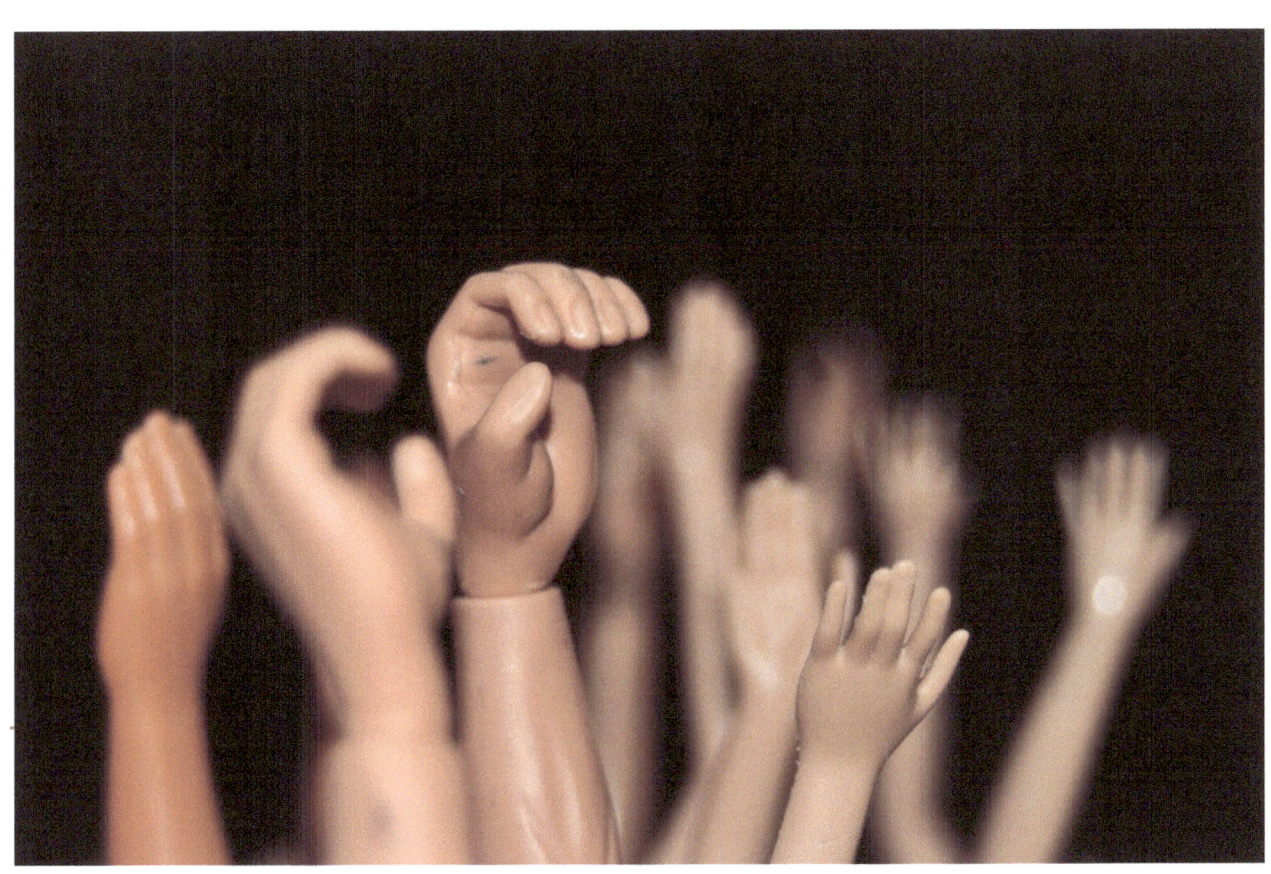

Beach Vacation

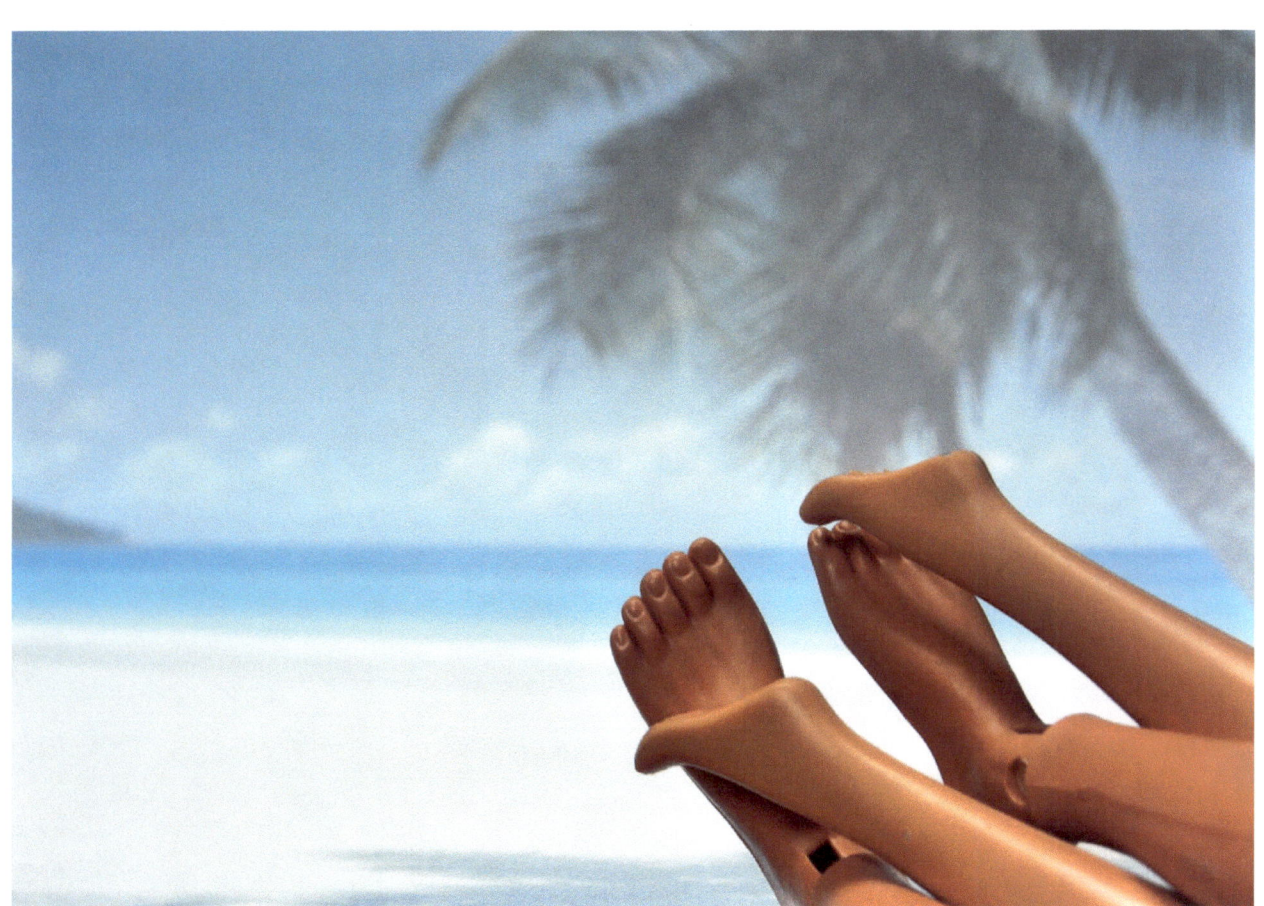

Sunken Treasure

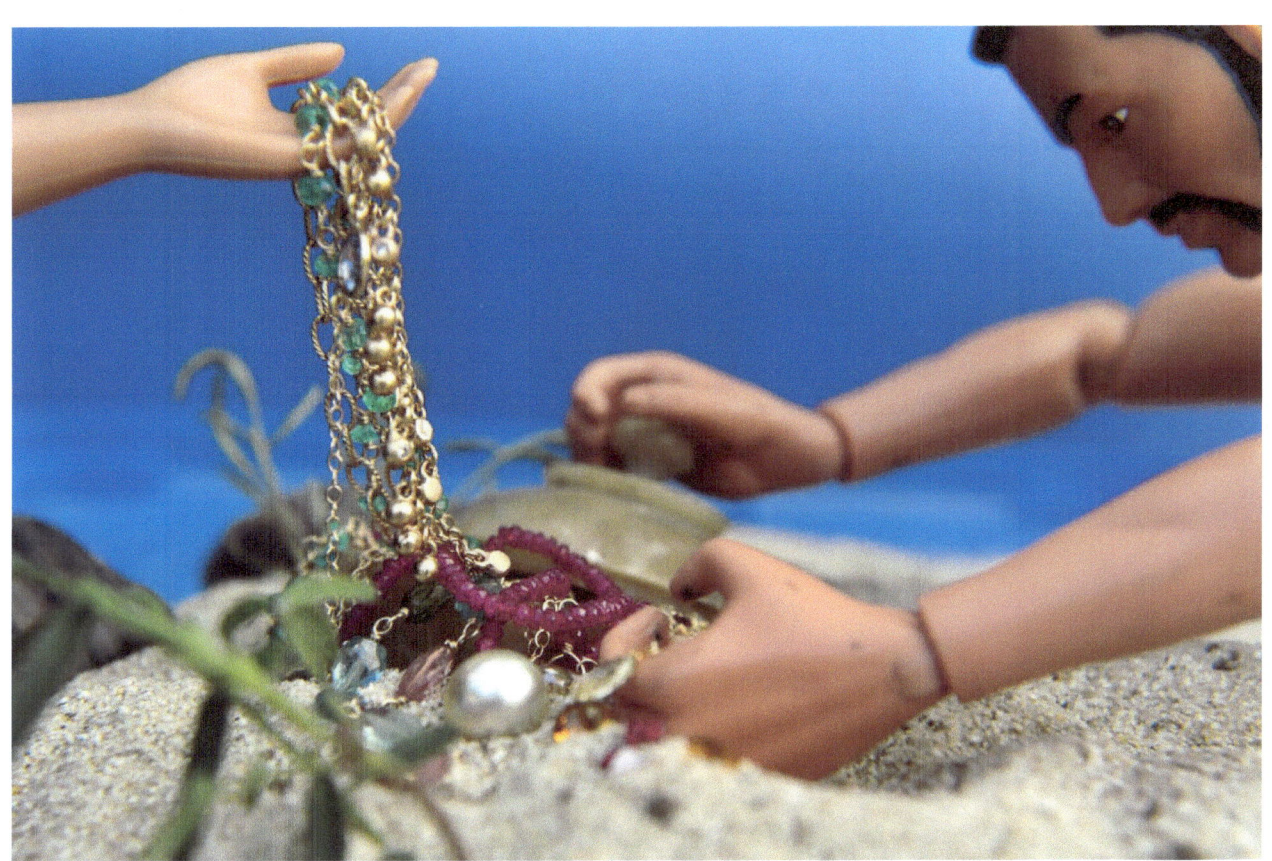

The Phone Is Ringing

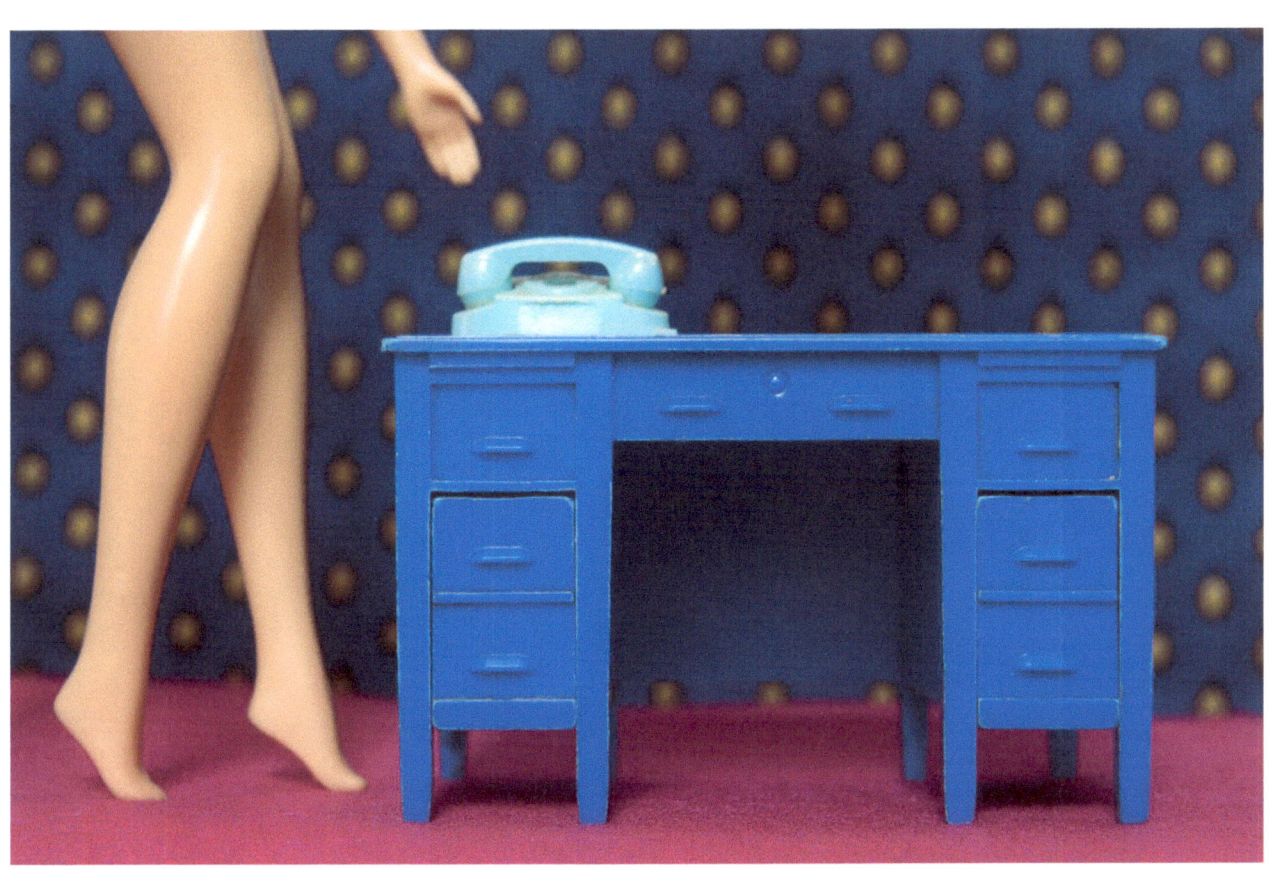

International Man Of Mystery

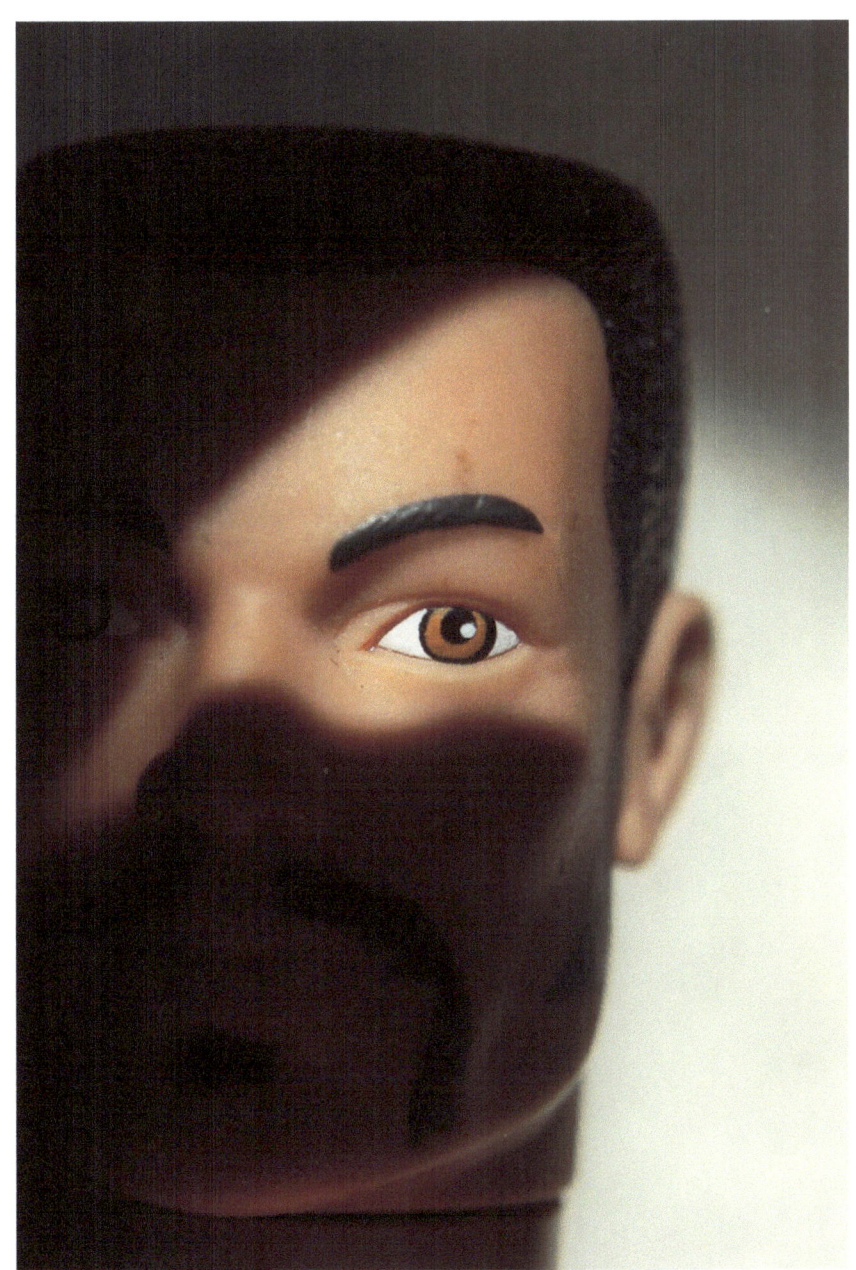

Princess & the Pea

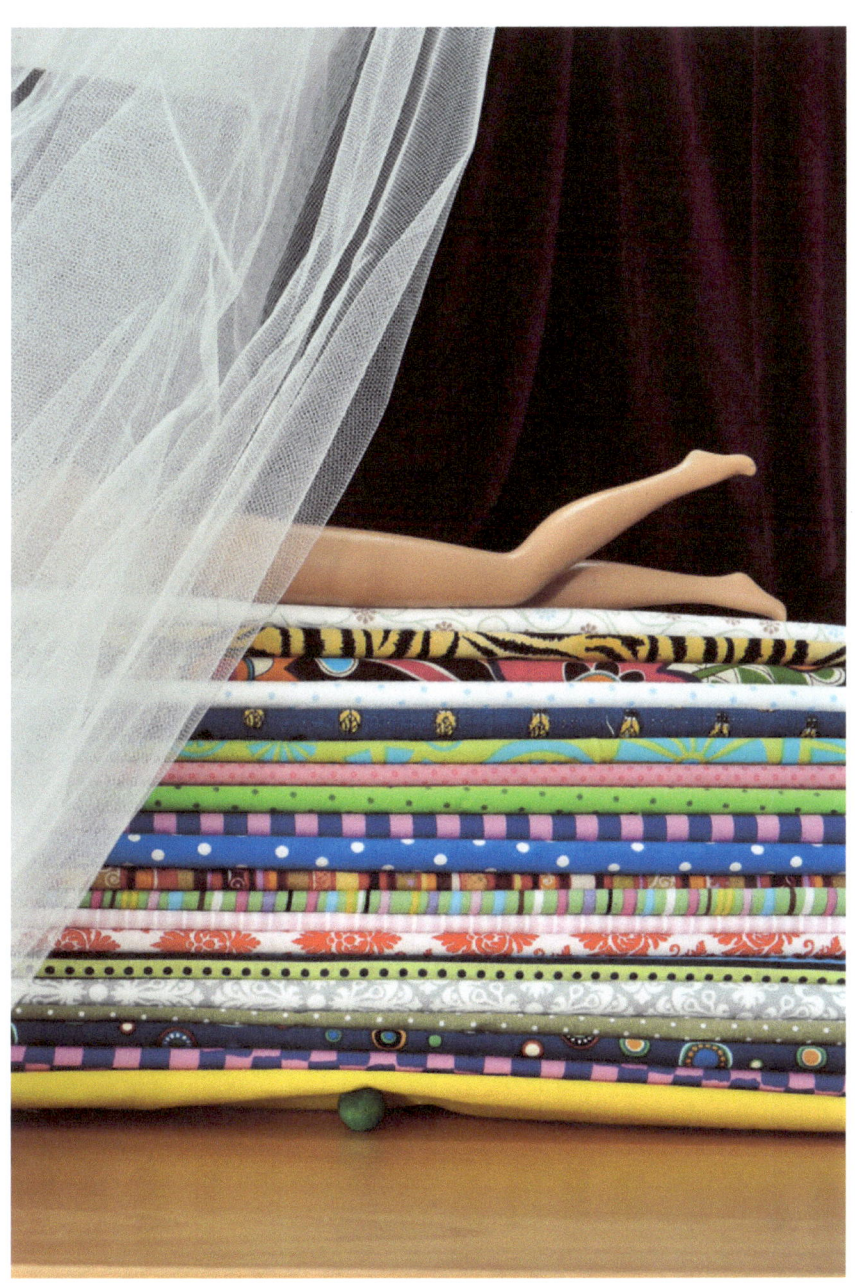

Romance Novel

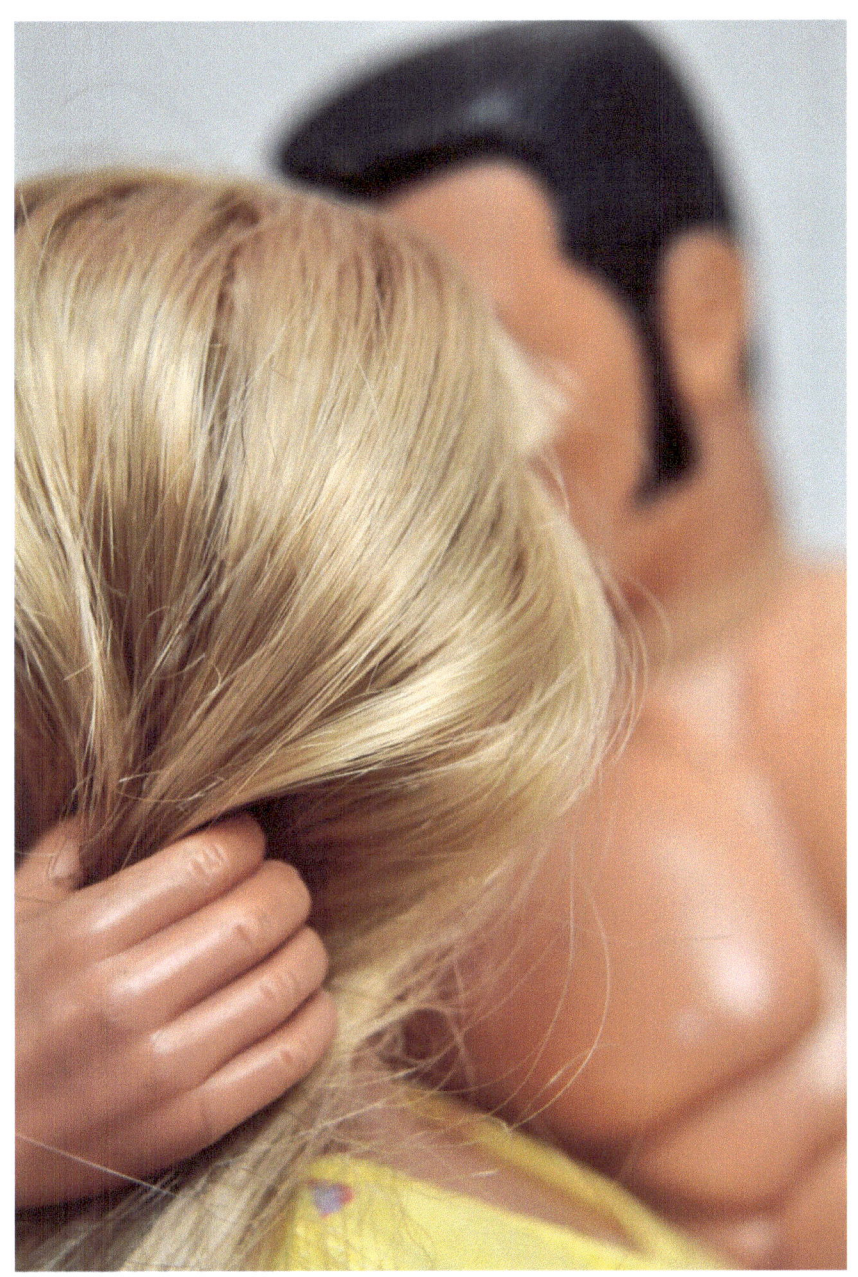

3 Graces

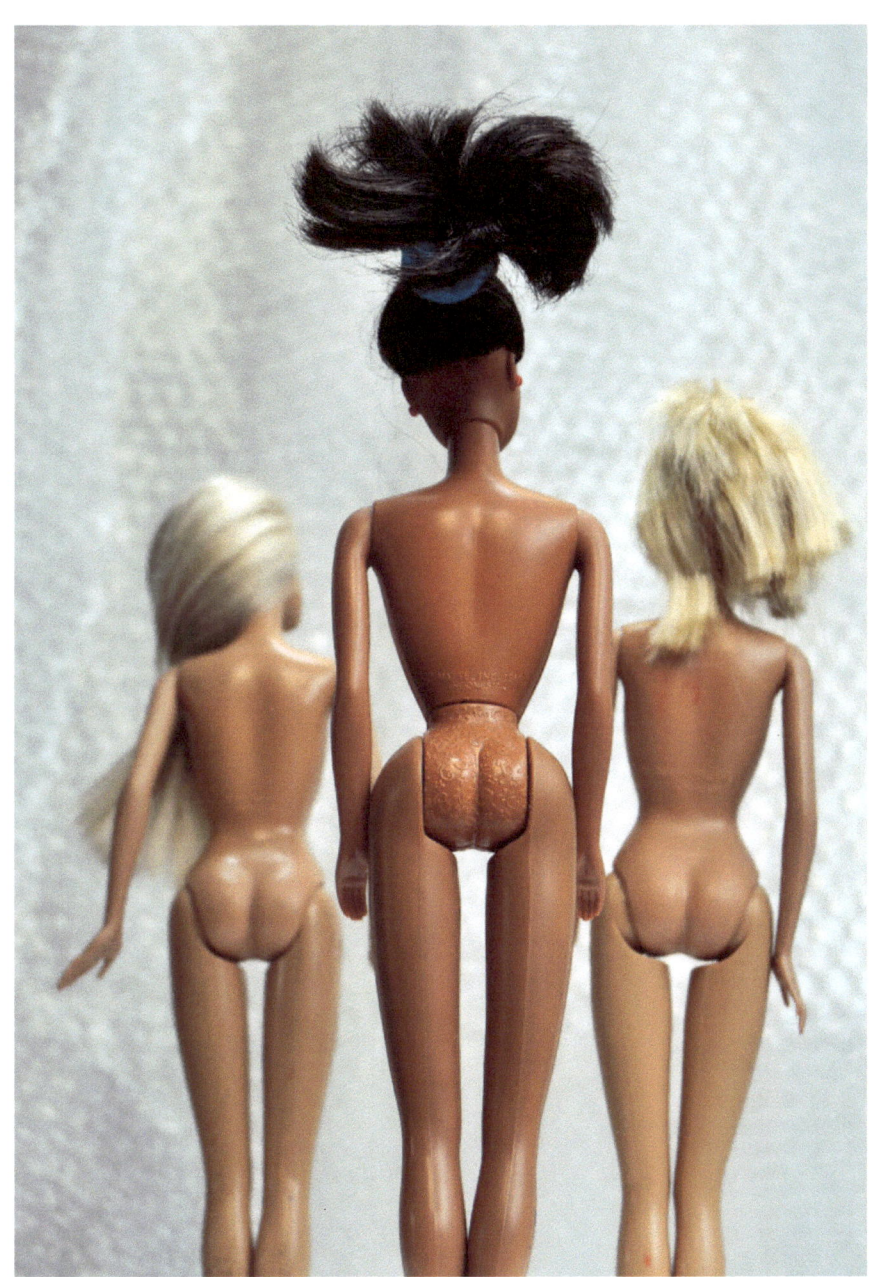

Joe's T Party

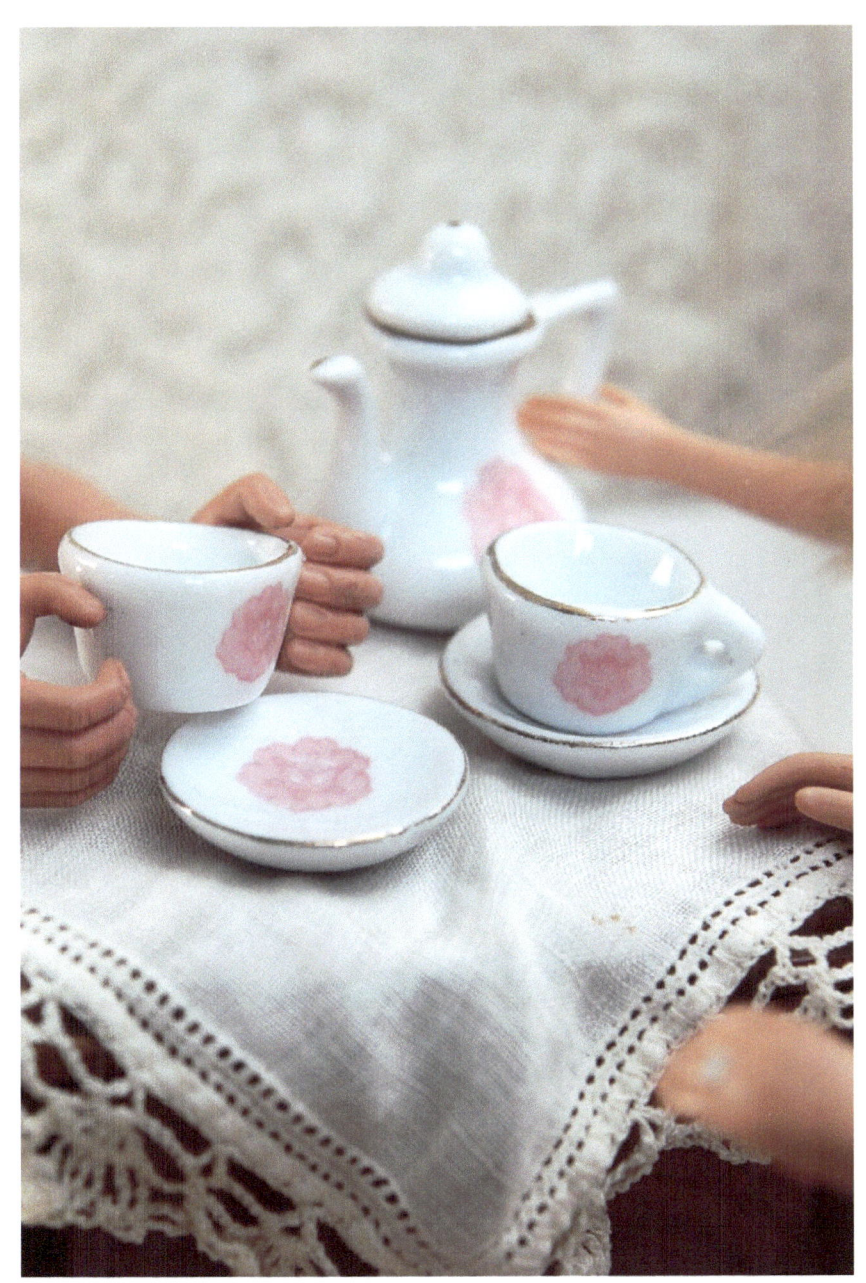

Seven

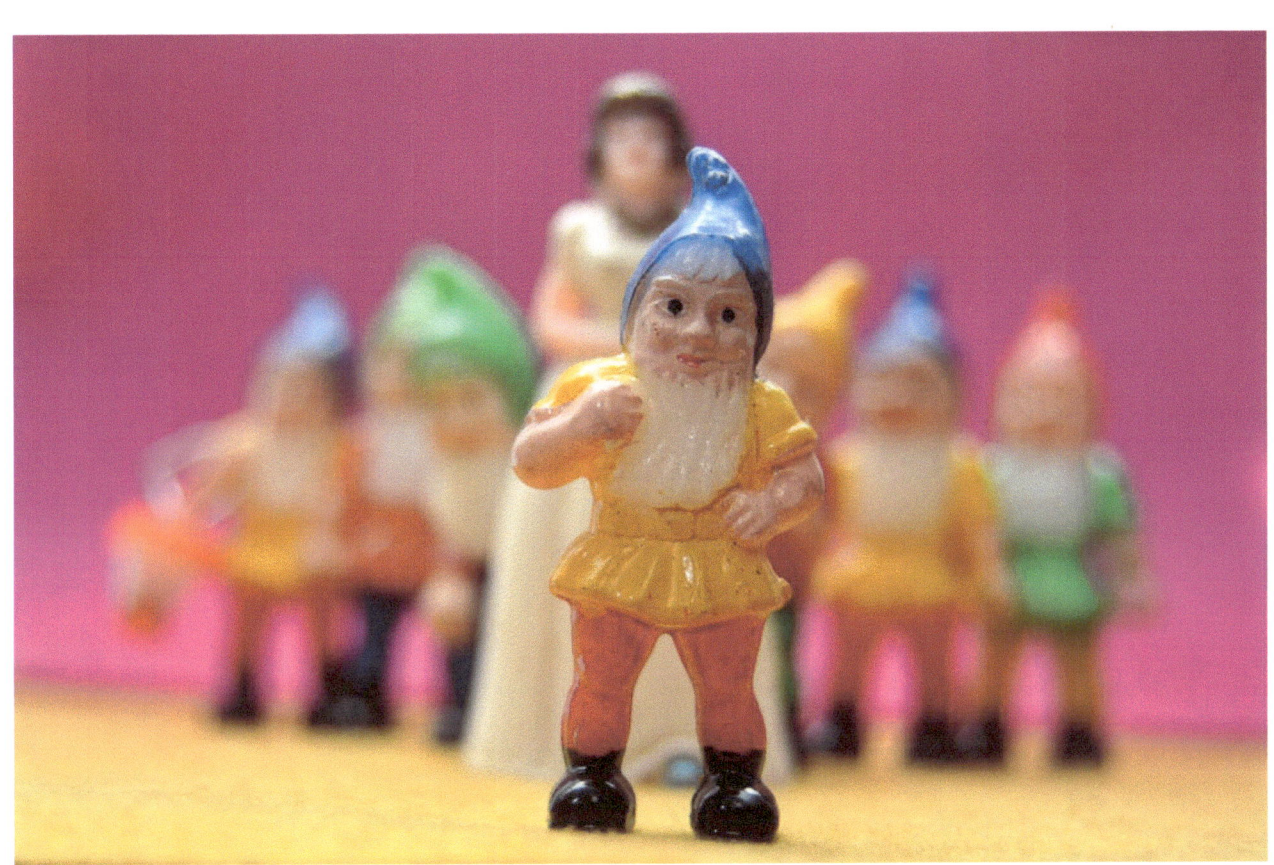

Uh-Oh Where's Phil?

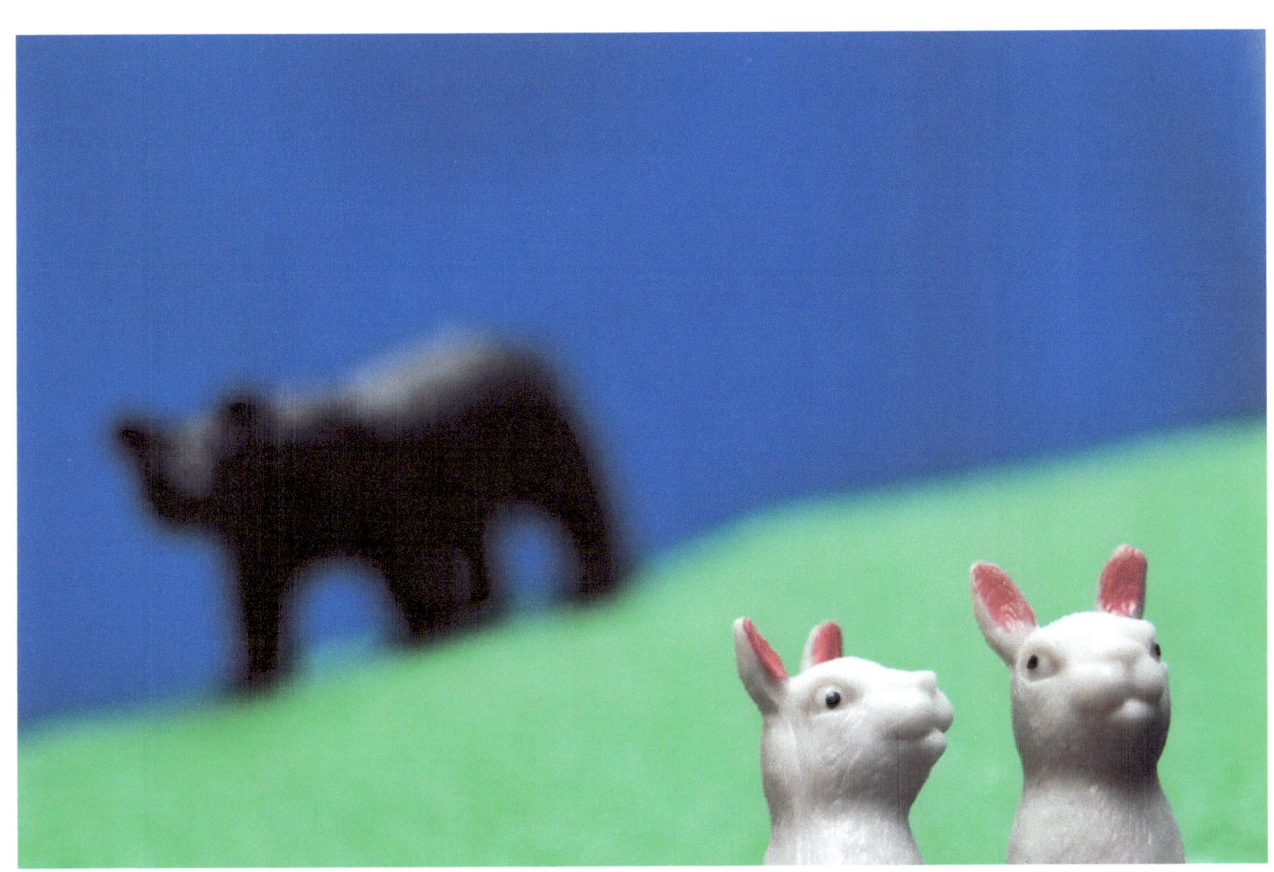

War With Chickens

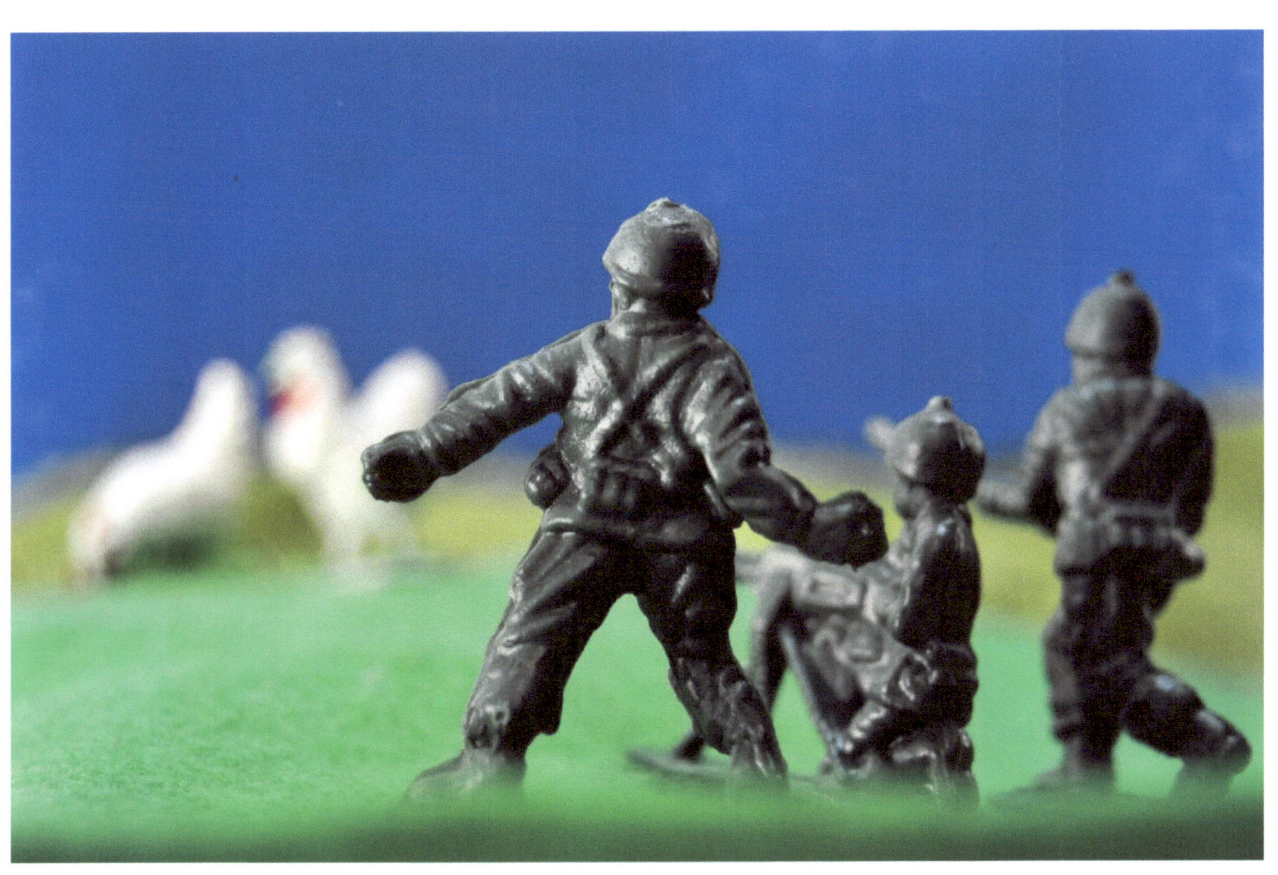

Dog Gaze

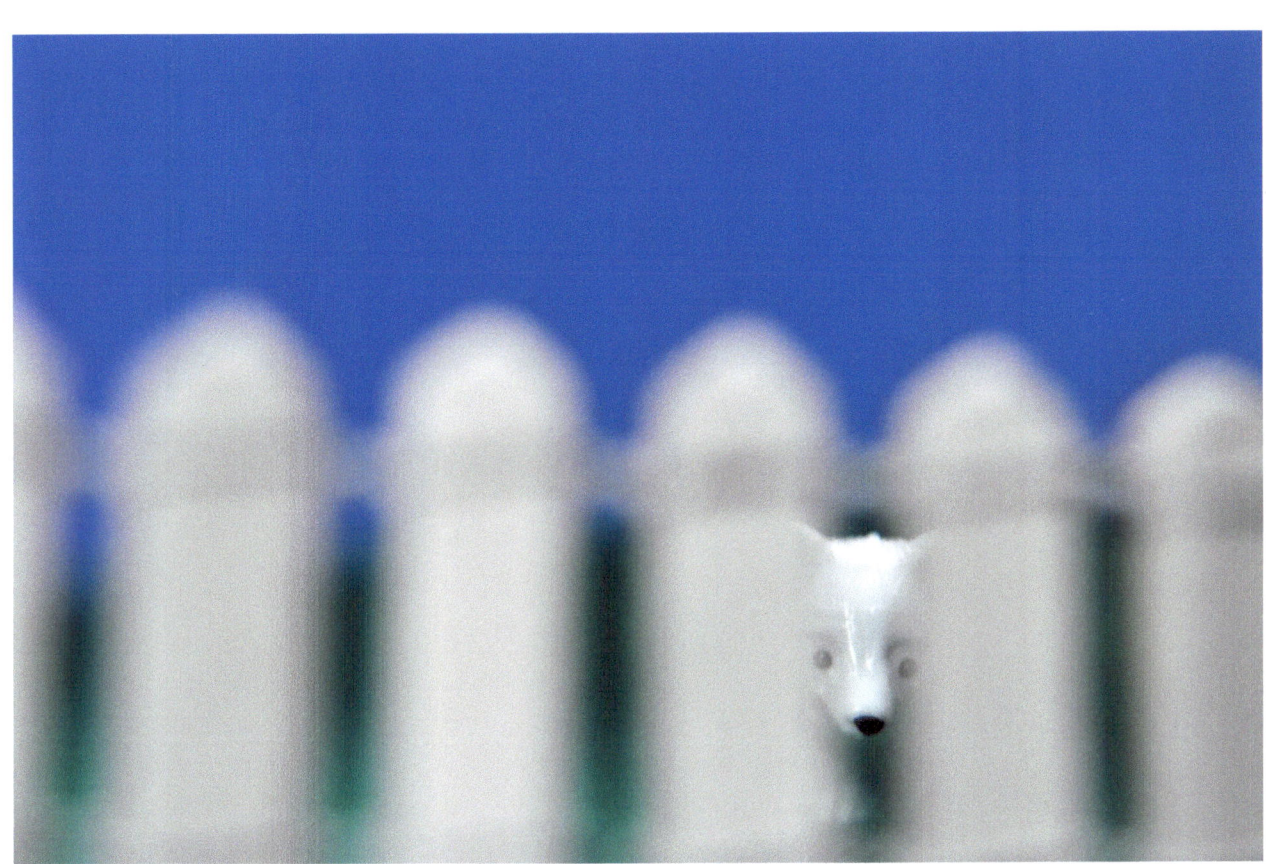

Pigs In Heaven

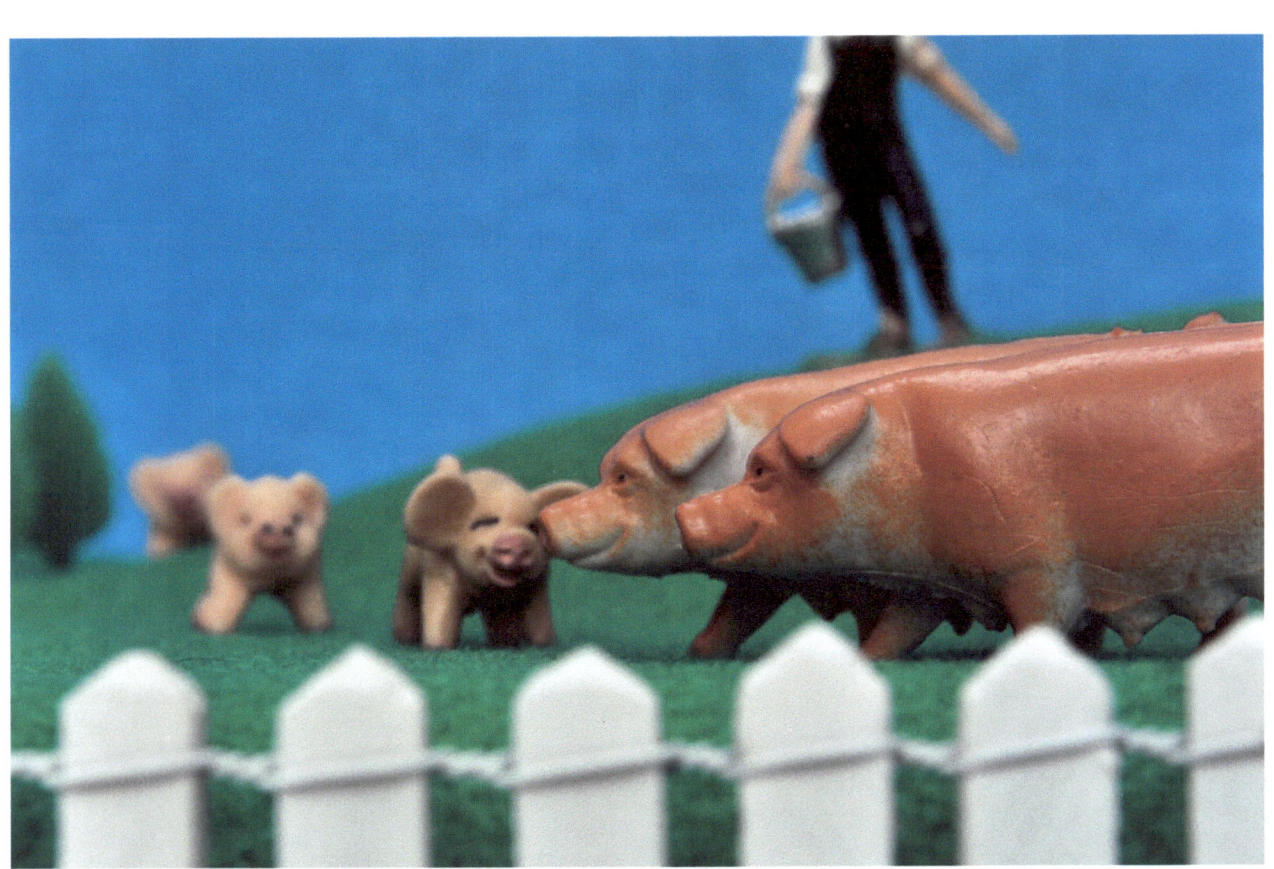

Choosey Bunnies

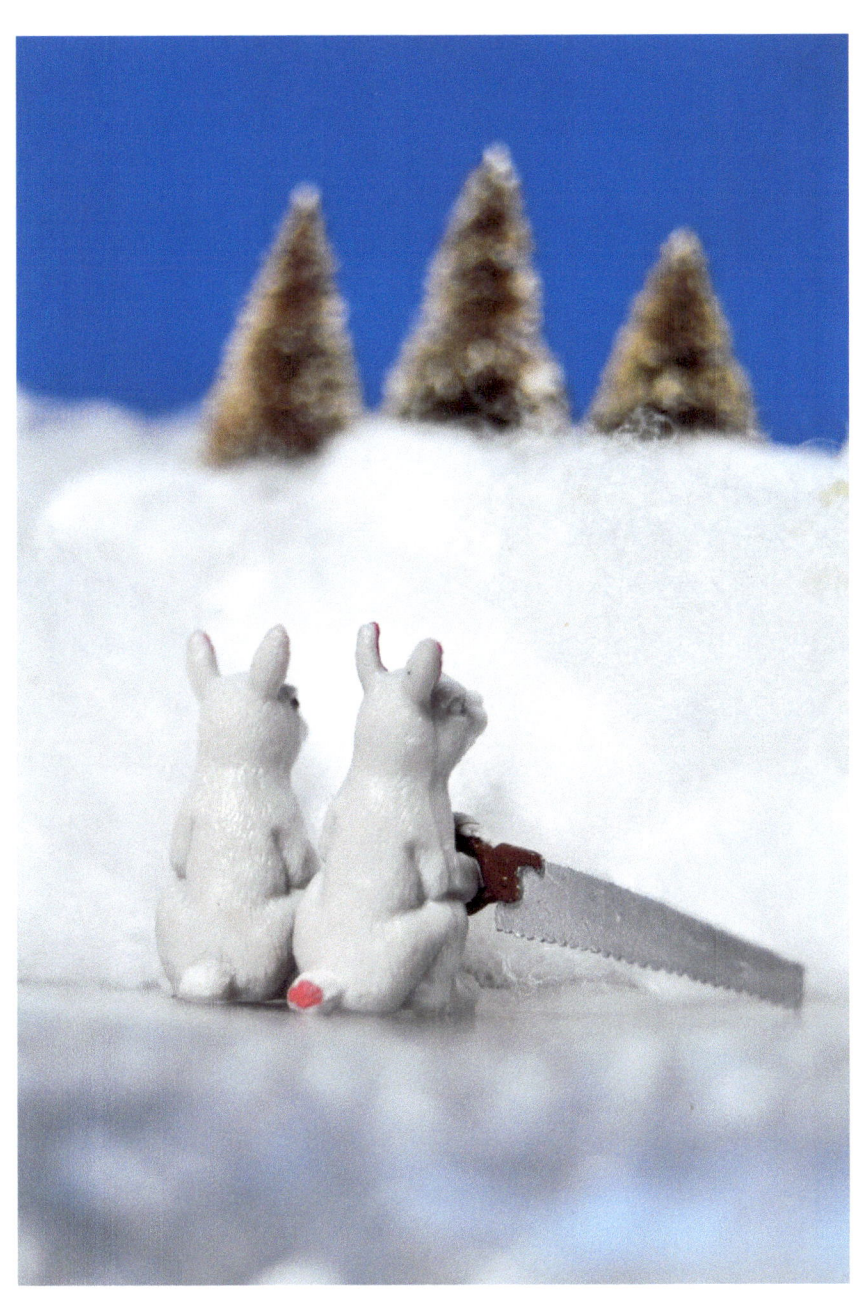

Up North

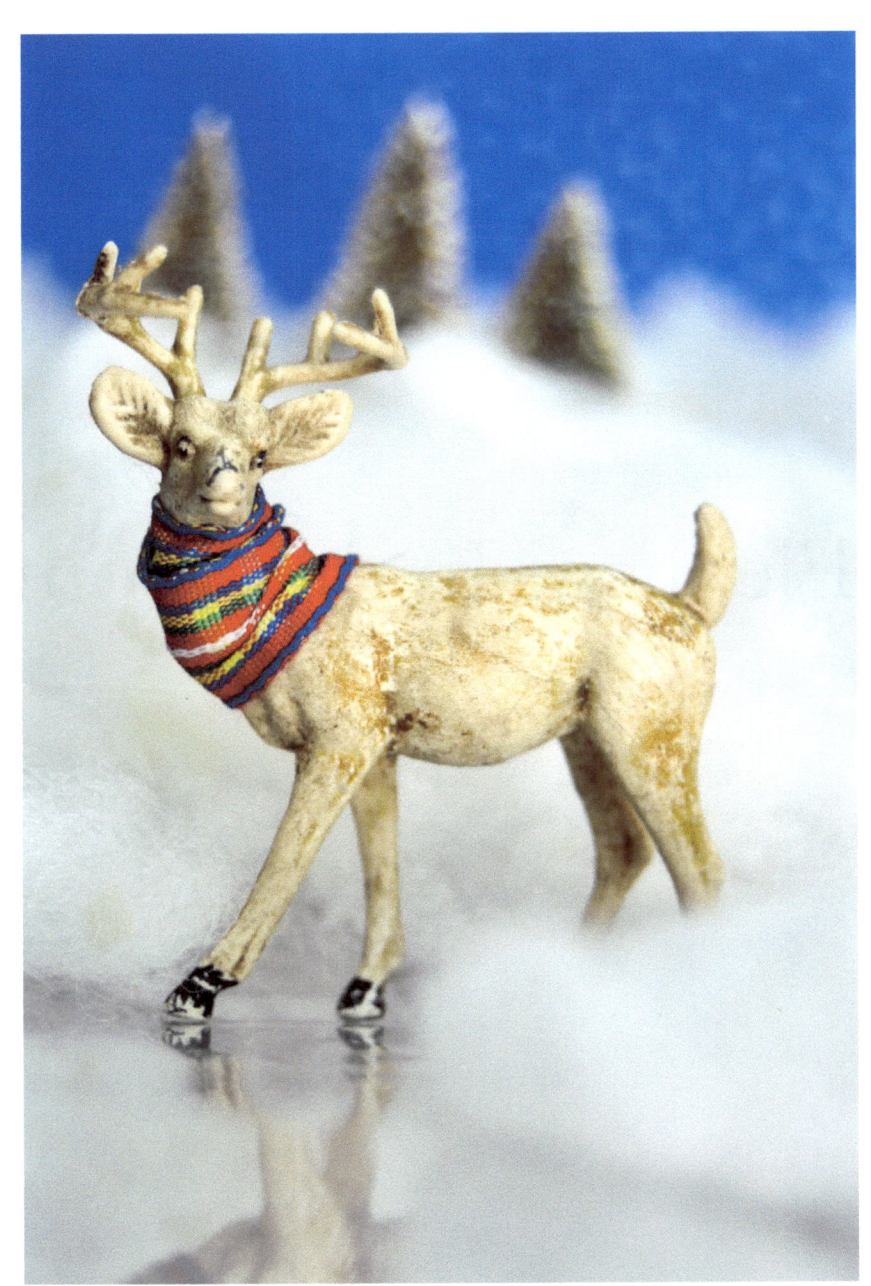

Elephant In the Room

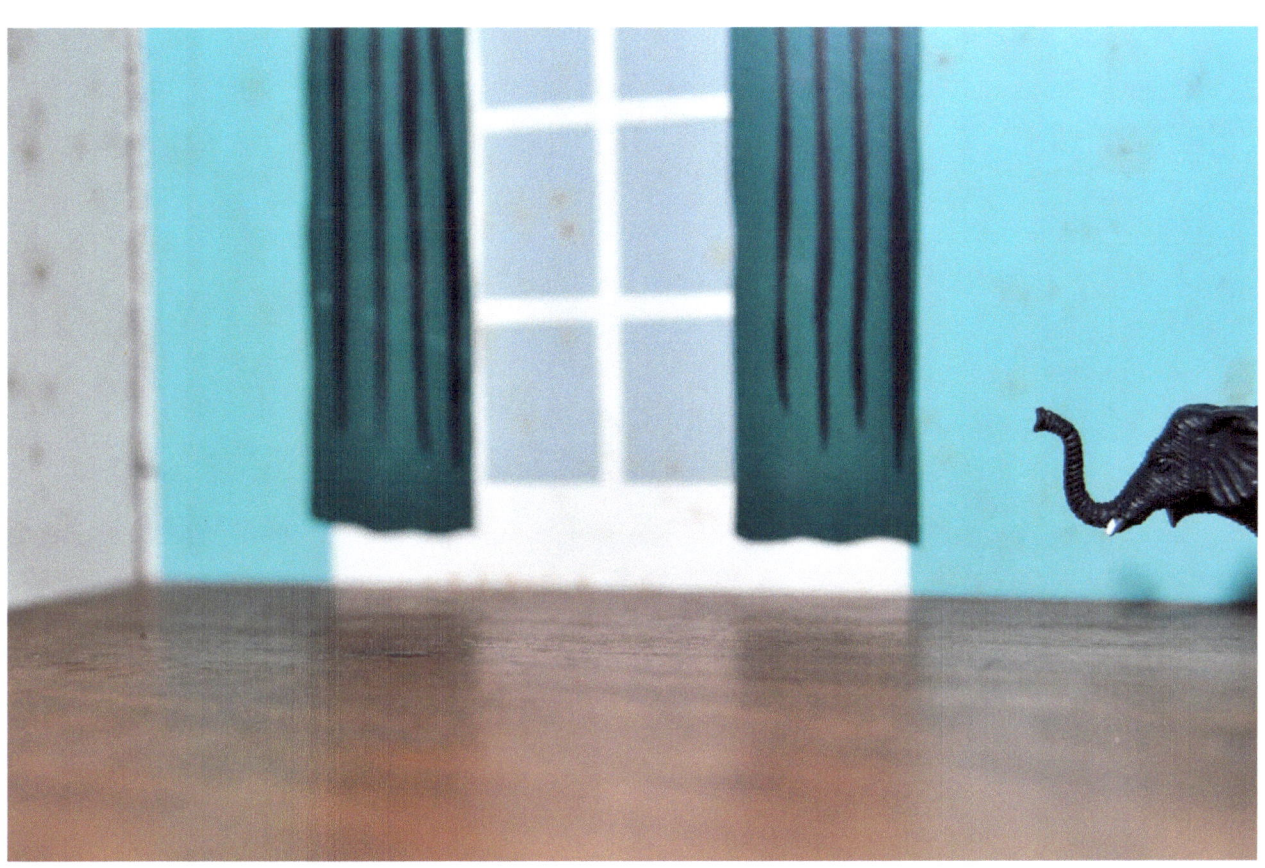

Paradise TV

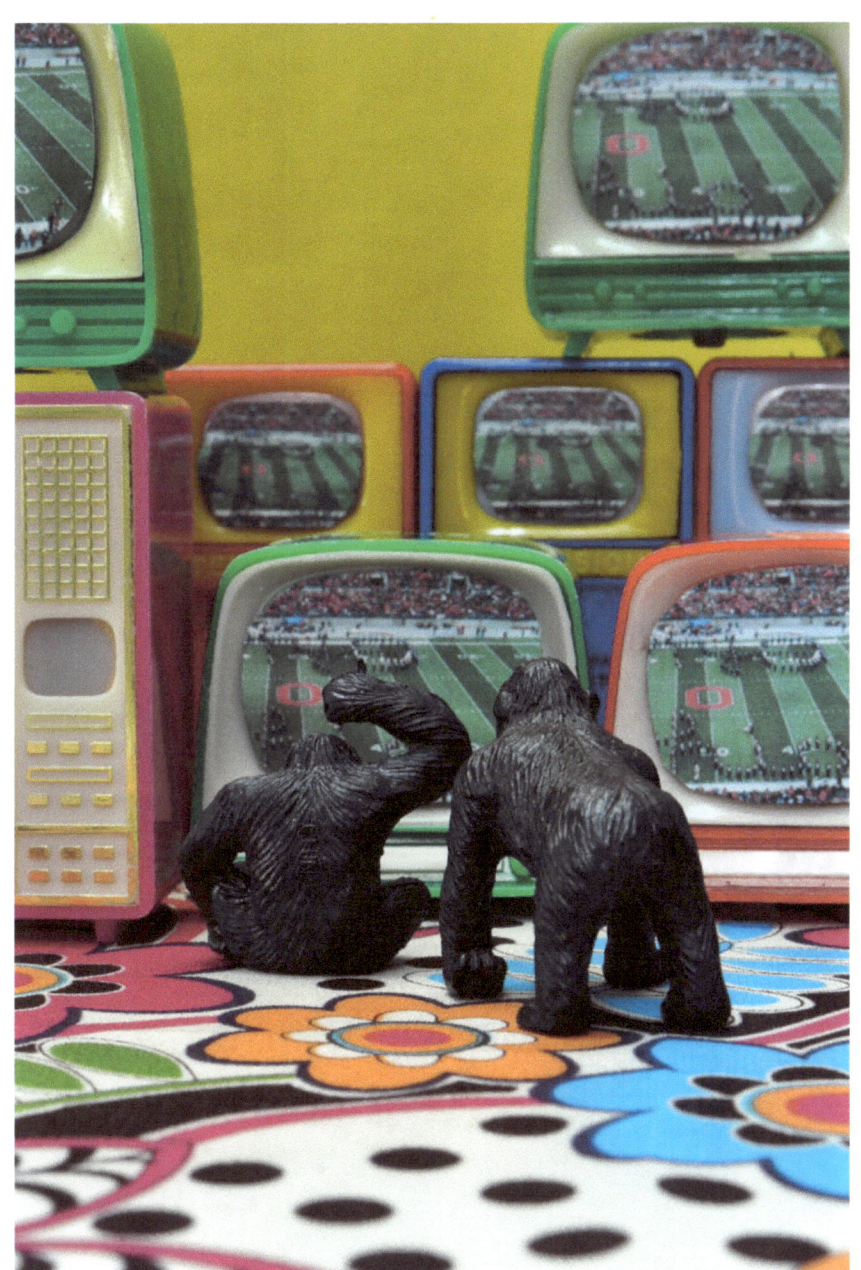

First And Ten

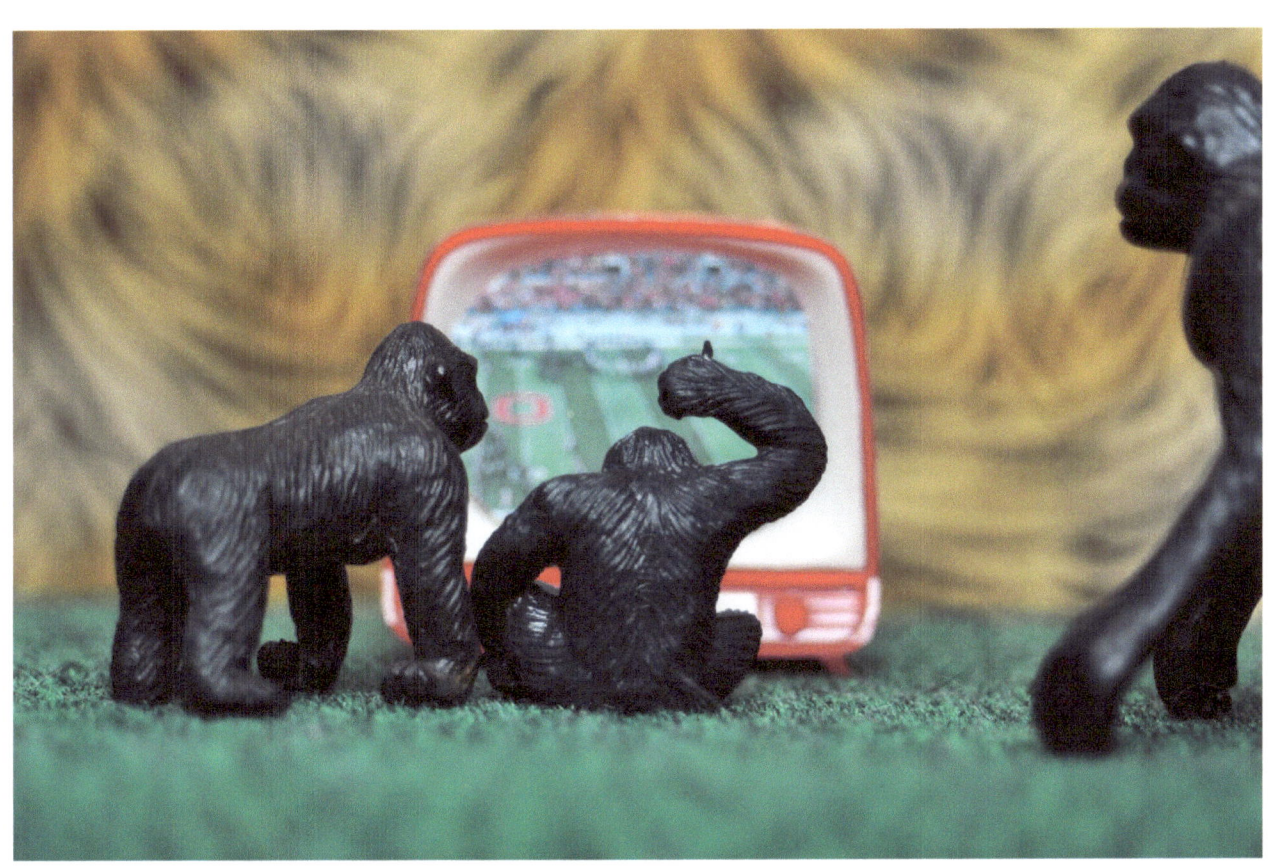

In the Pink

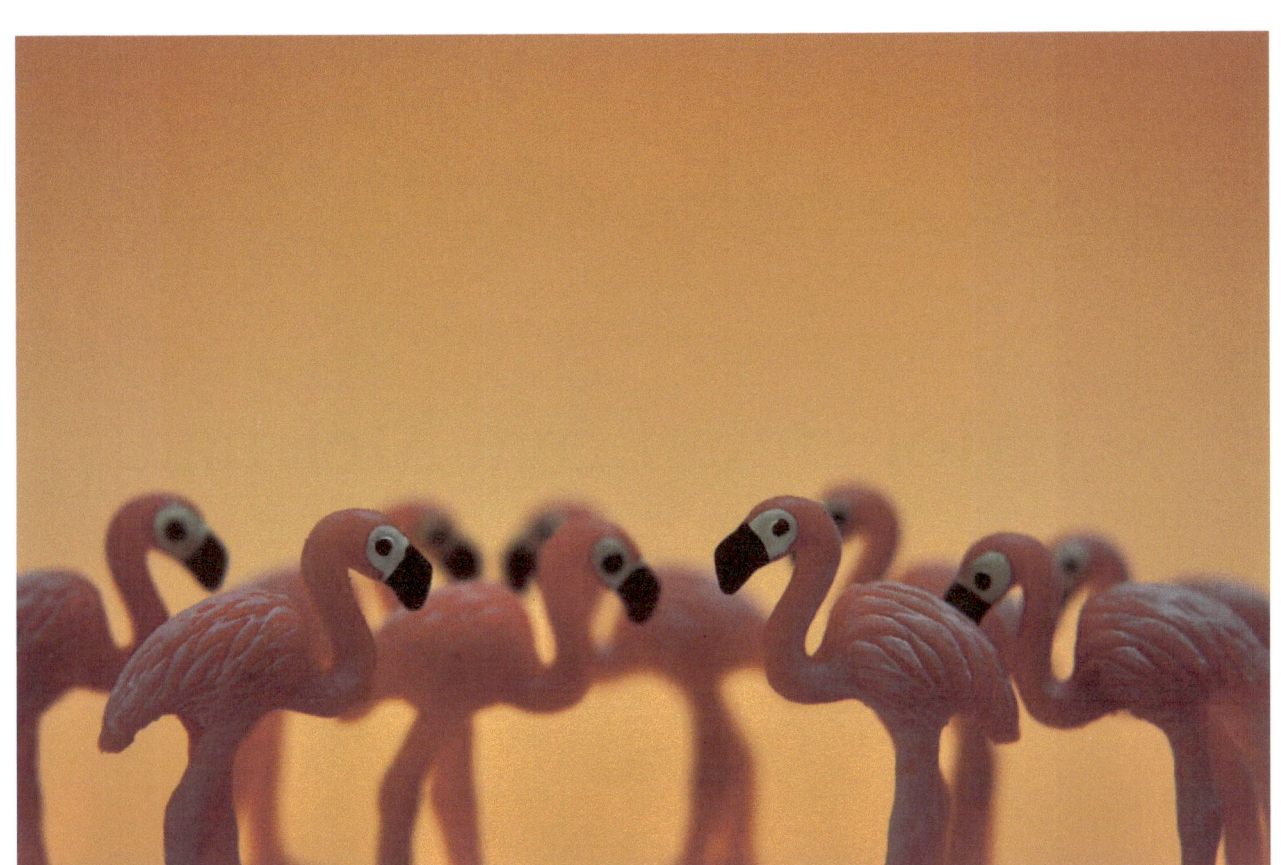

Sea Monsters Love Mermaids

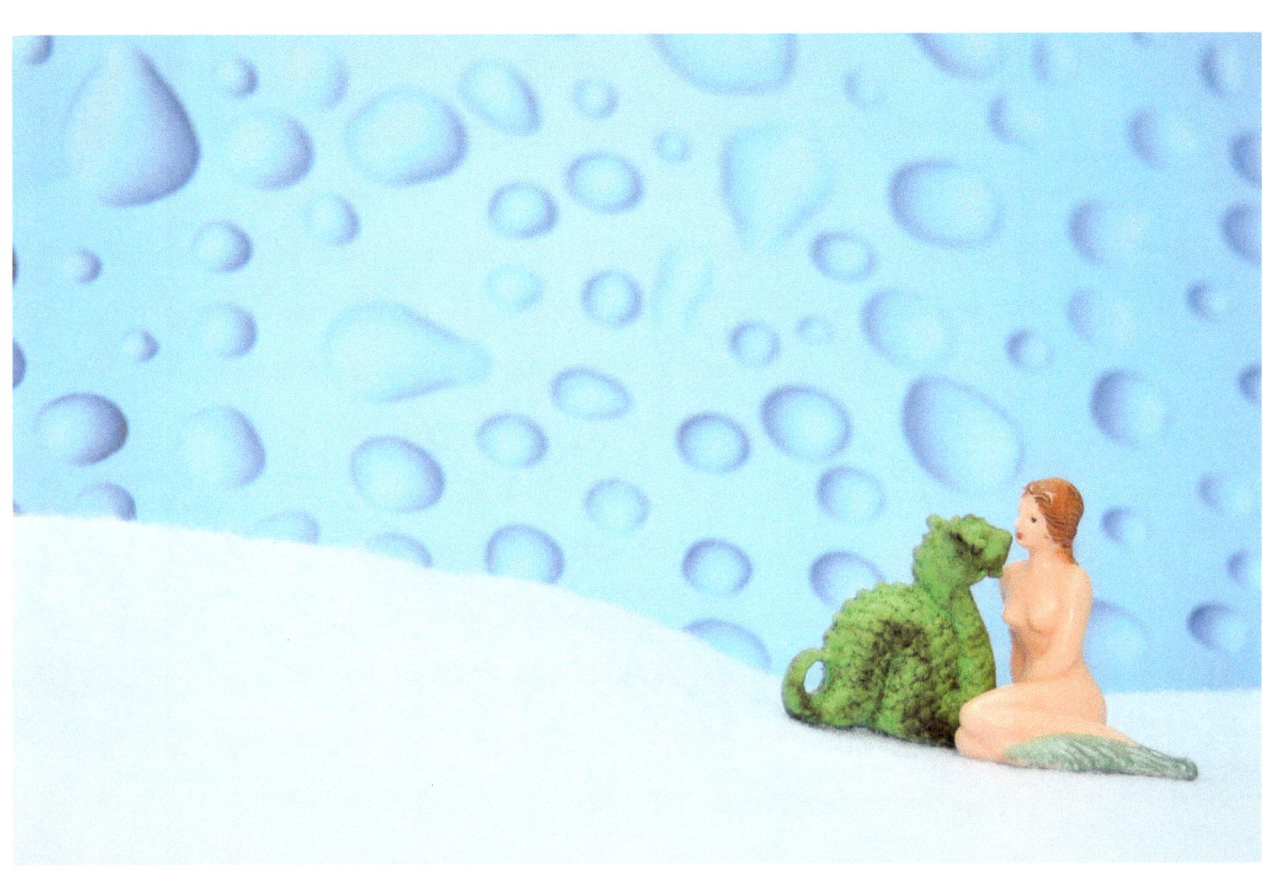

Lions, Tigers, Bears

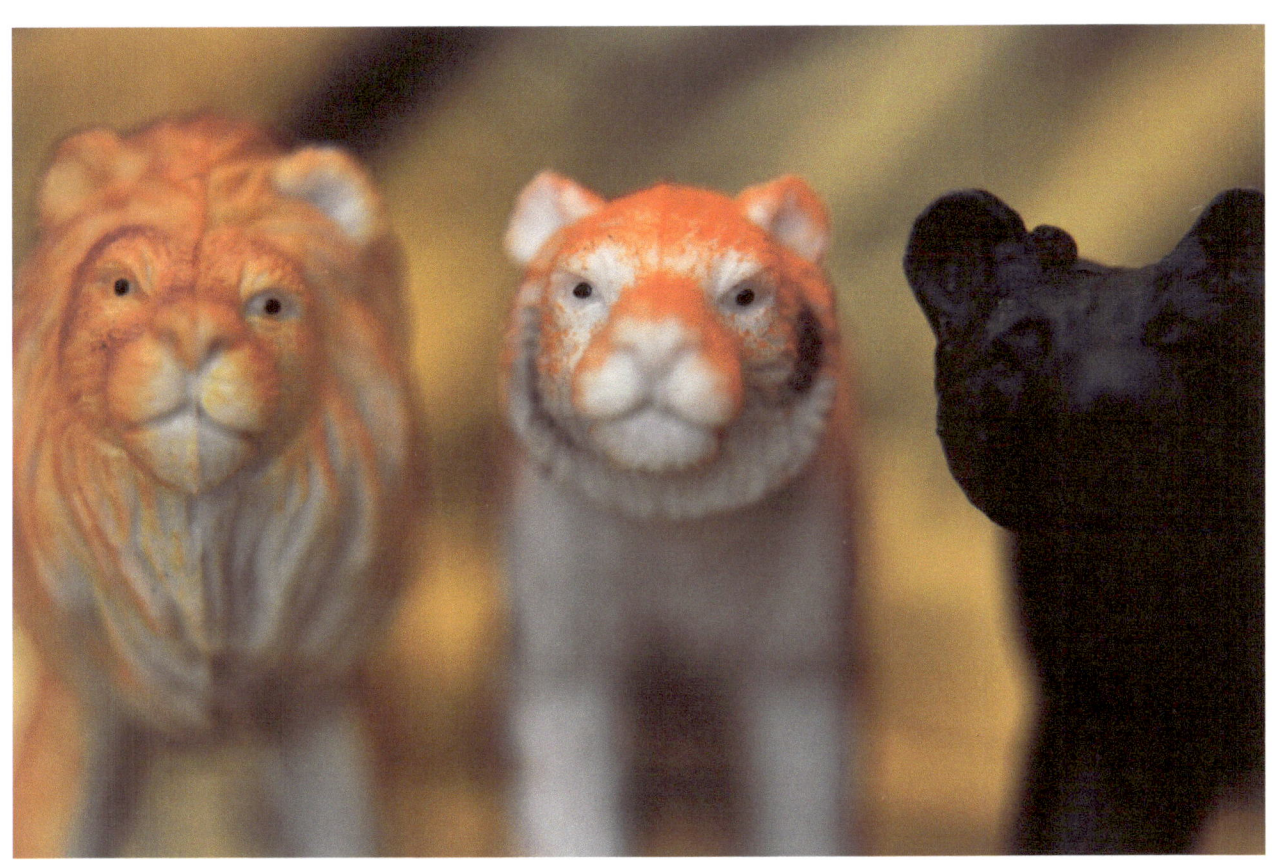

Super Petite Train

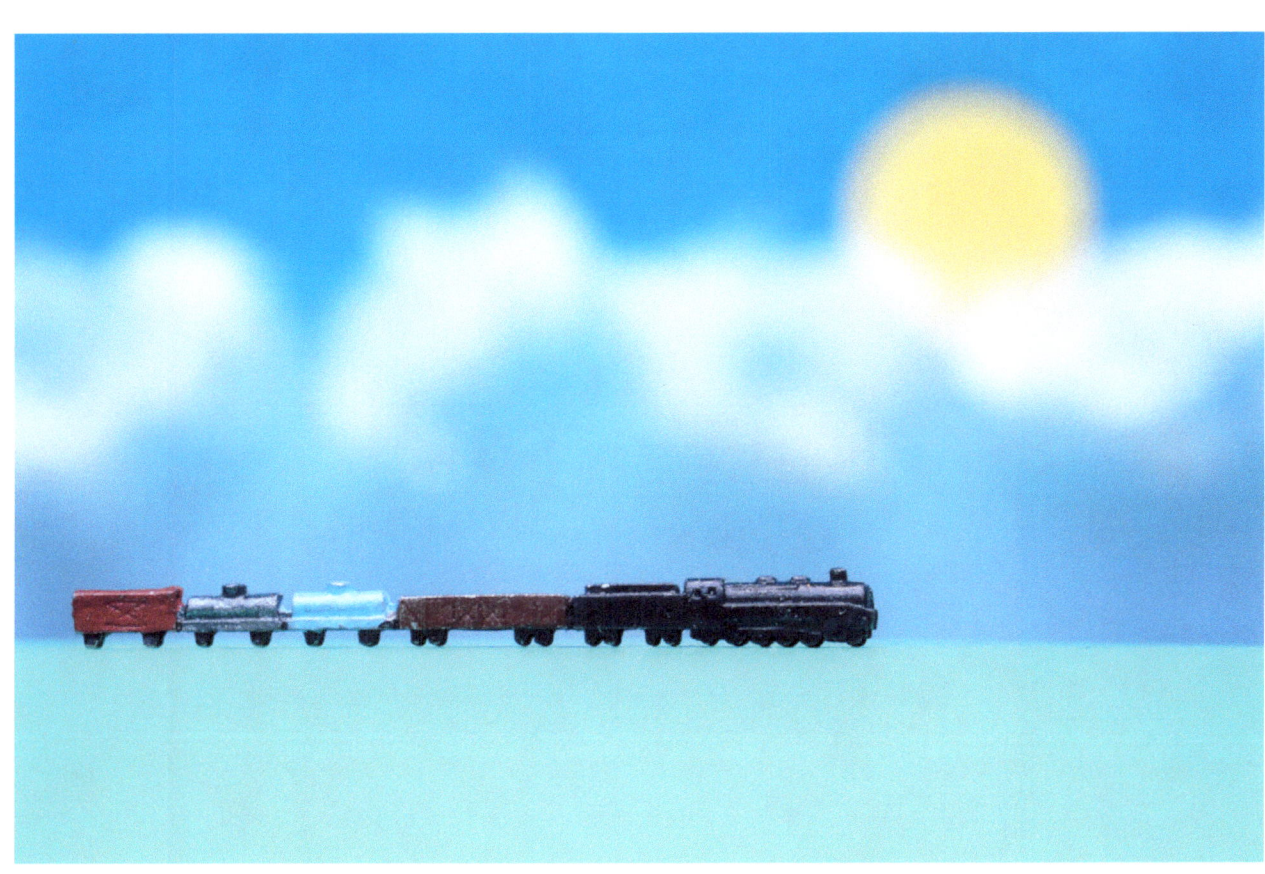

Kitchen Sink

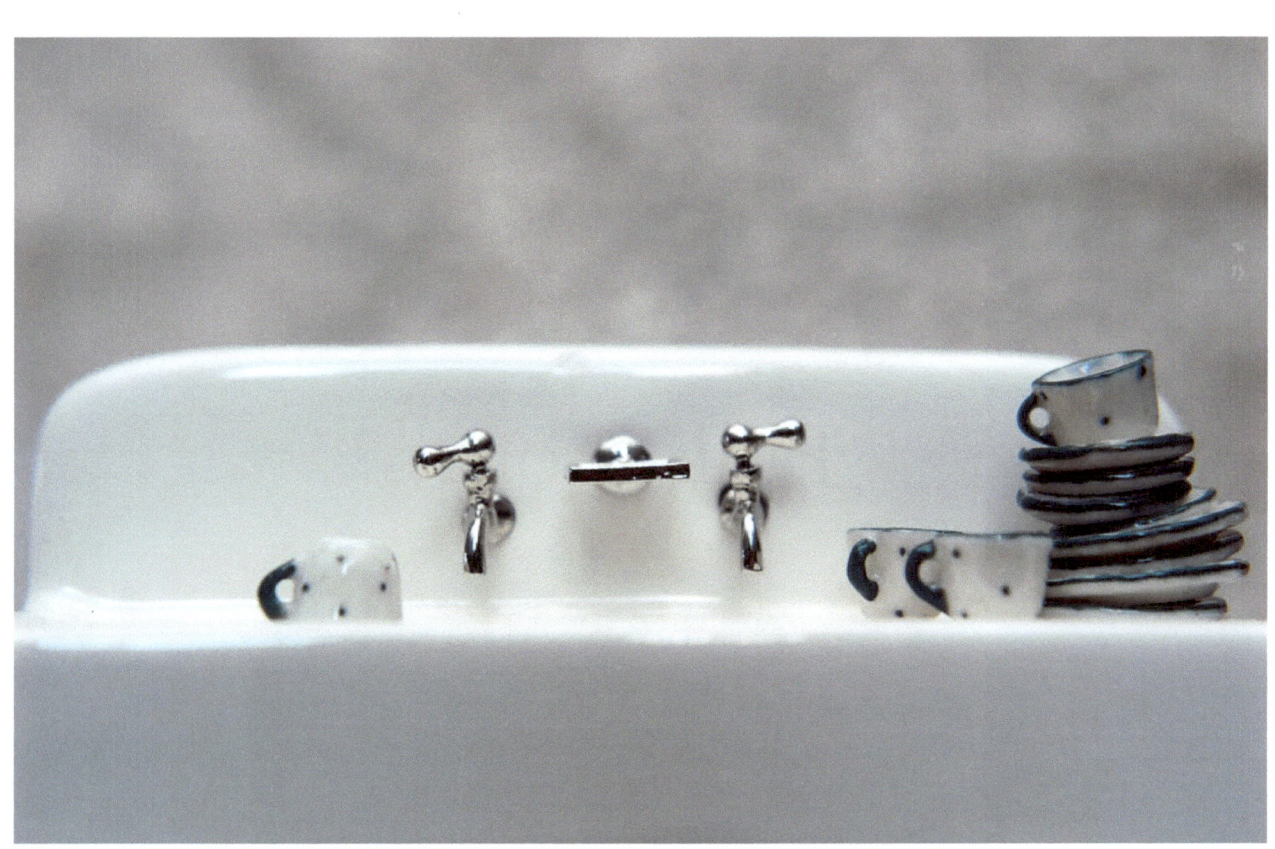

Pink Mom

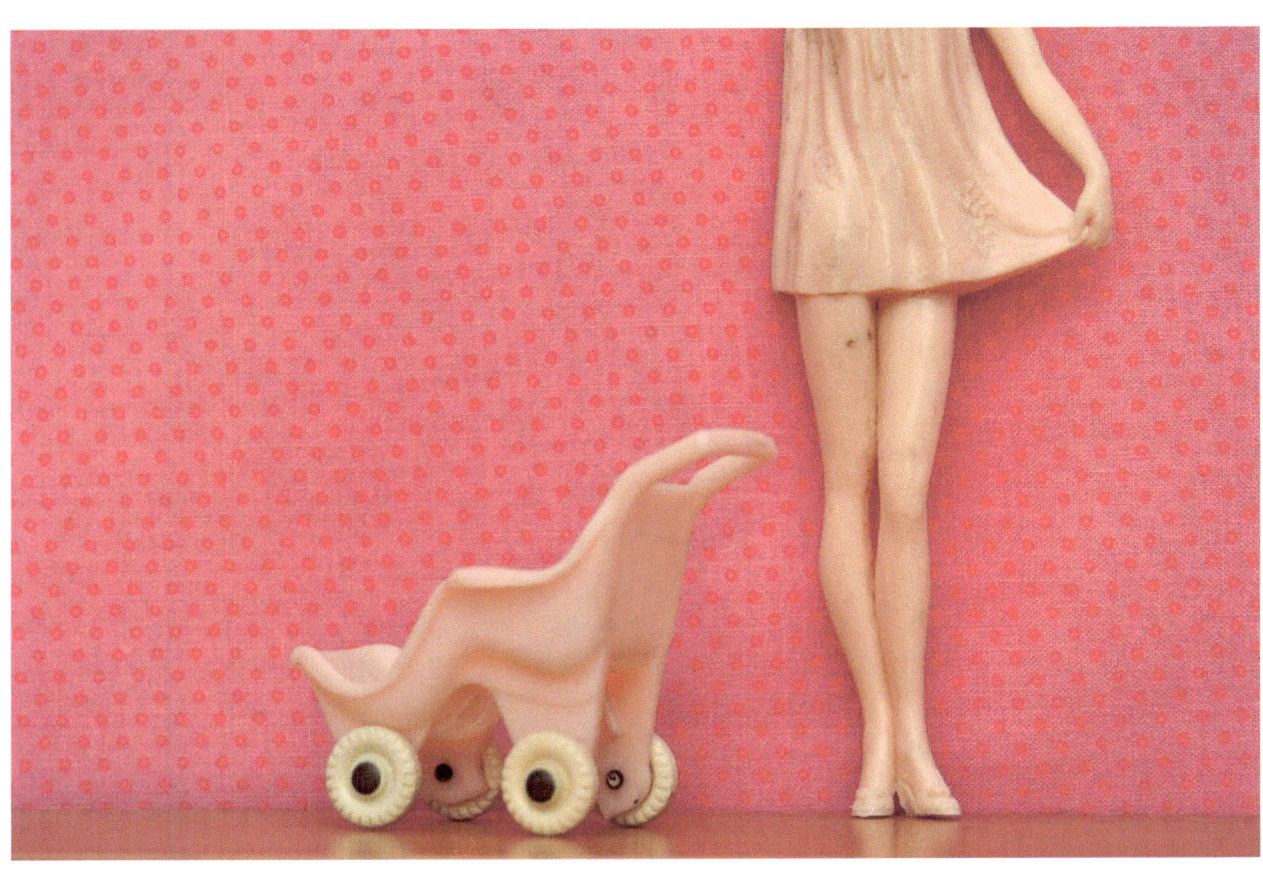

Putting Out Fires

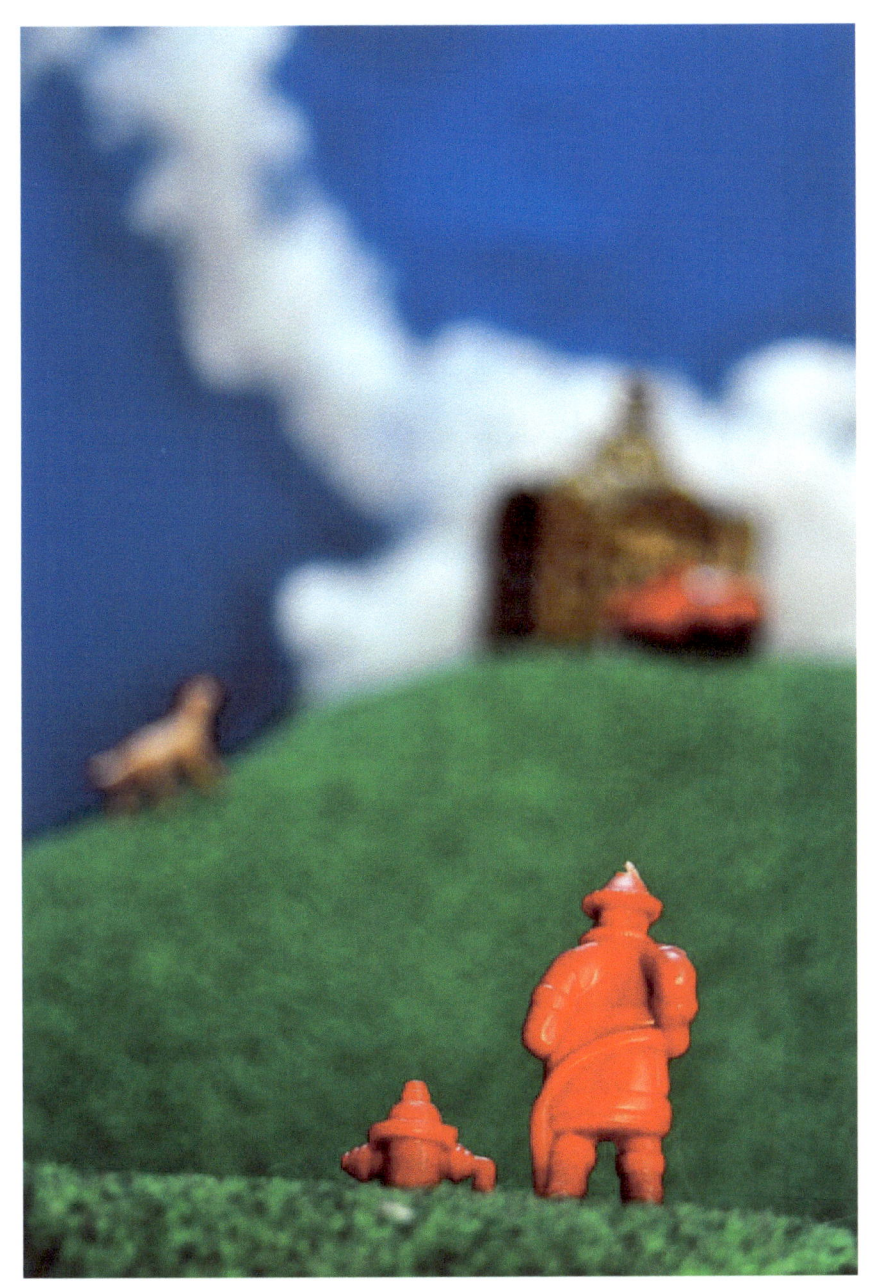

Mistaken Identities

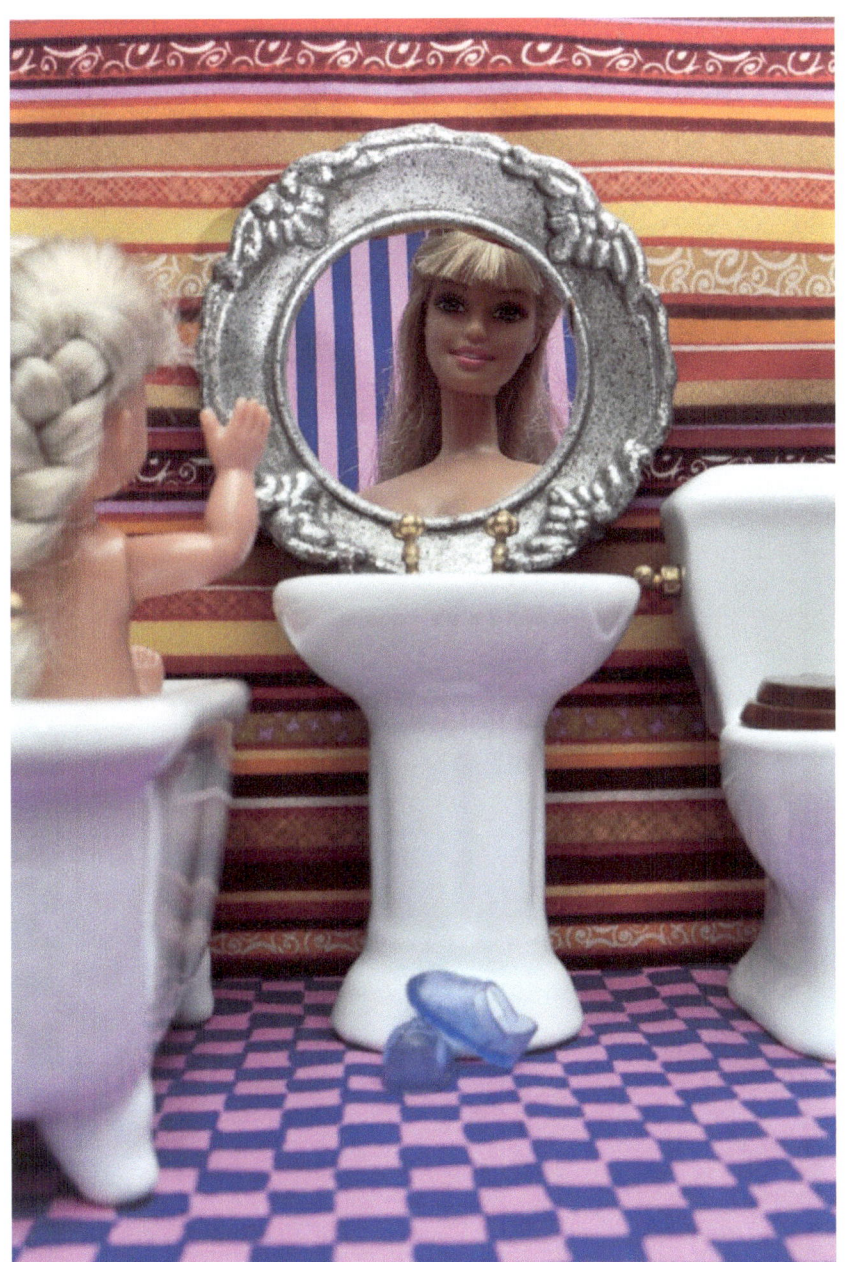

Multi Tasking

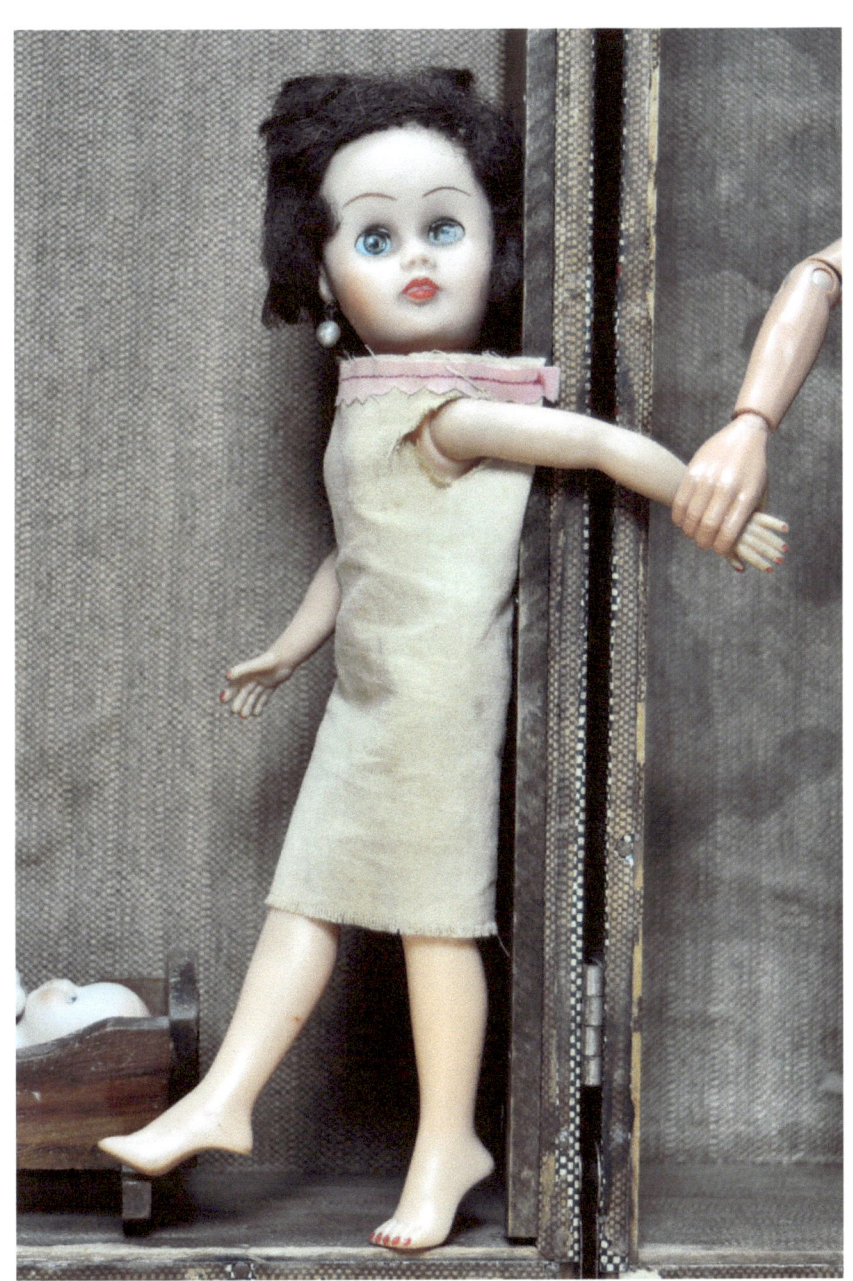

Yellow Ribbon

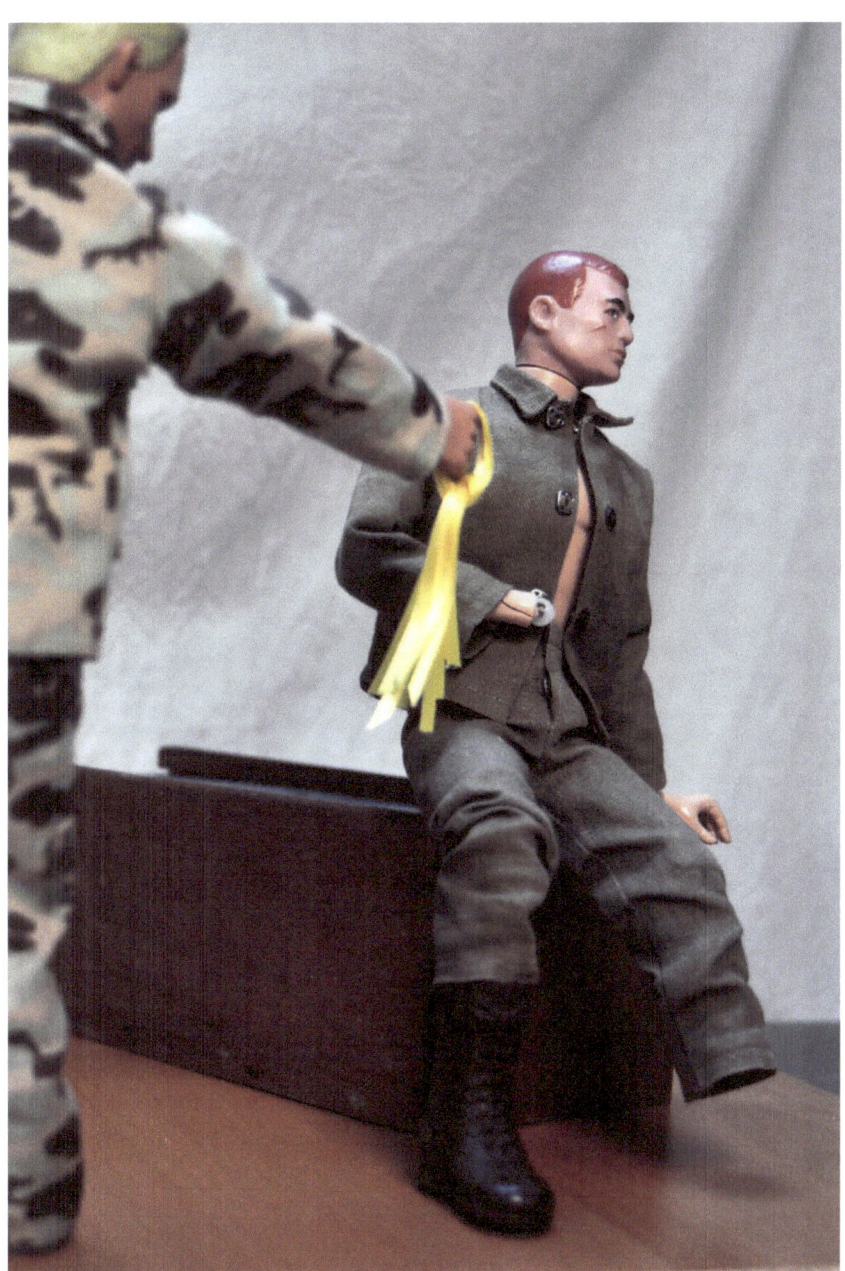

Full Moon

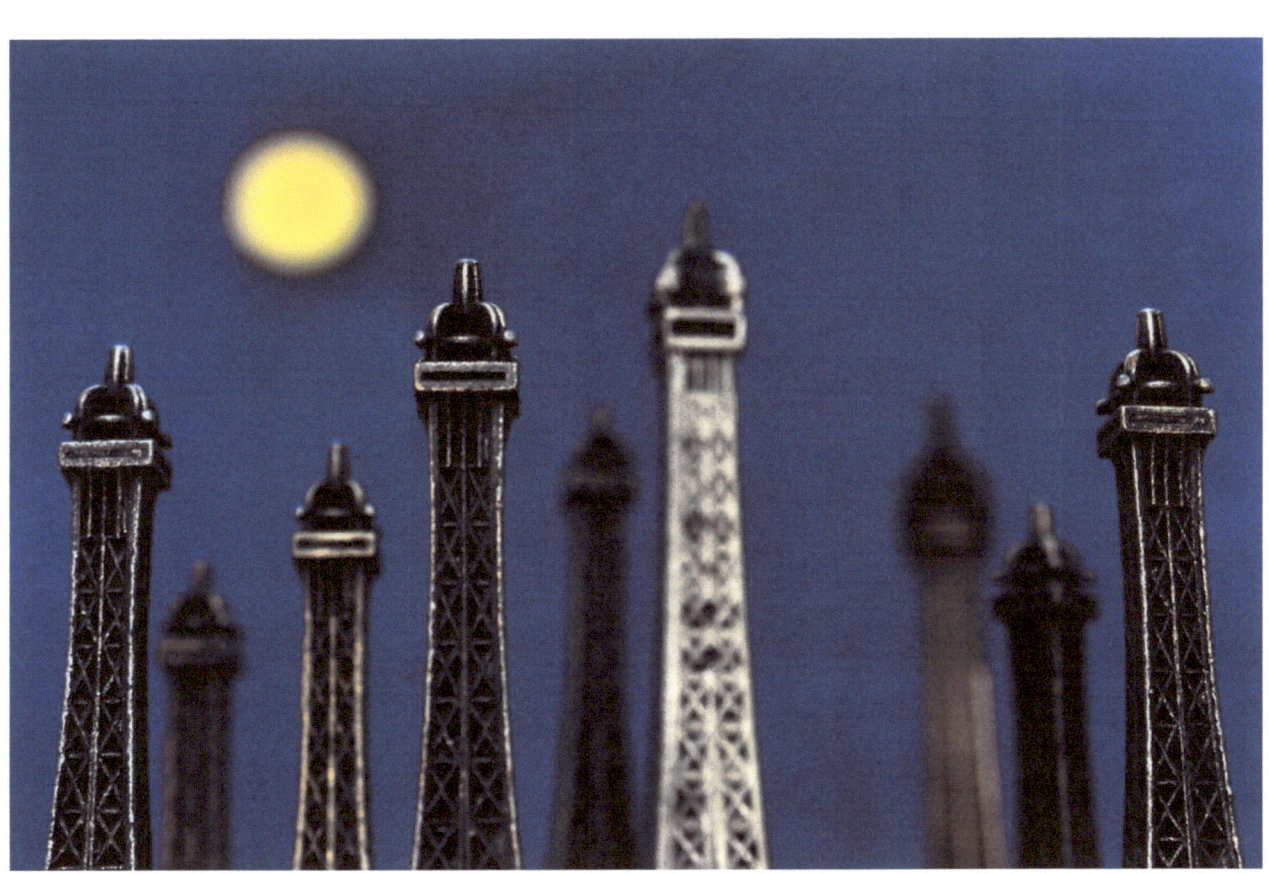

Paris Fog

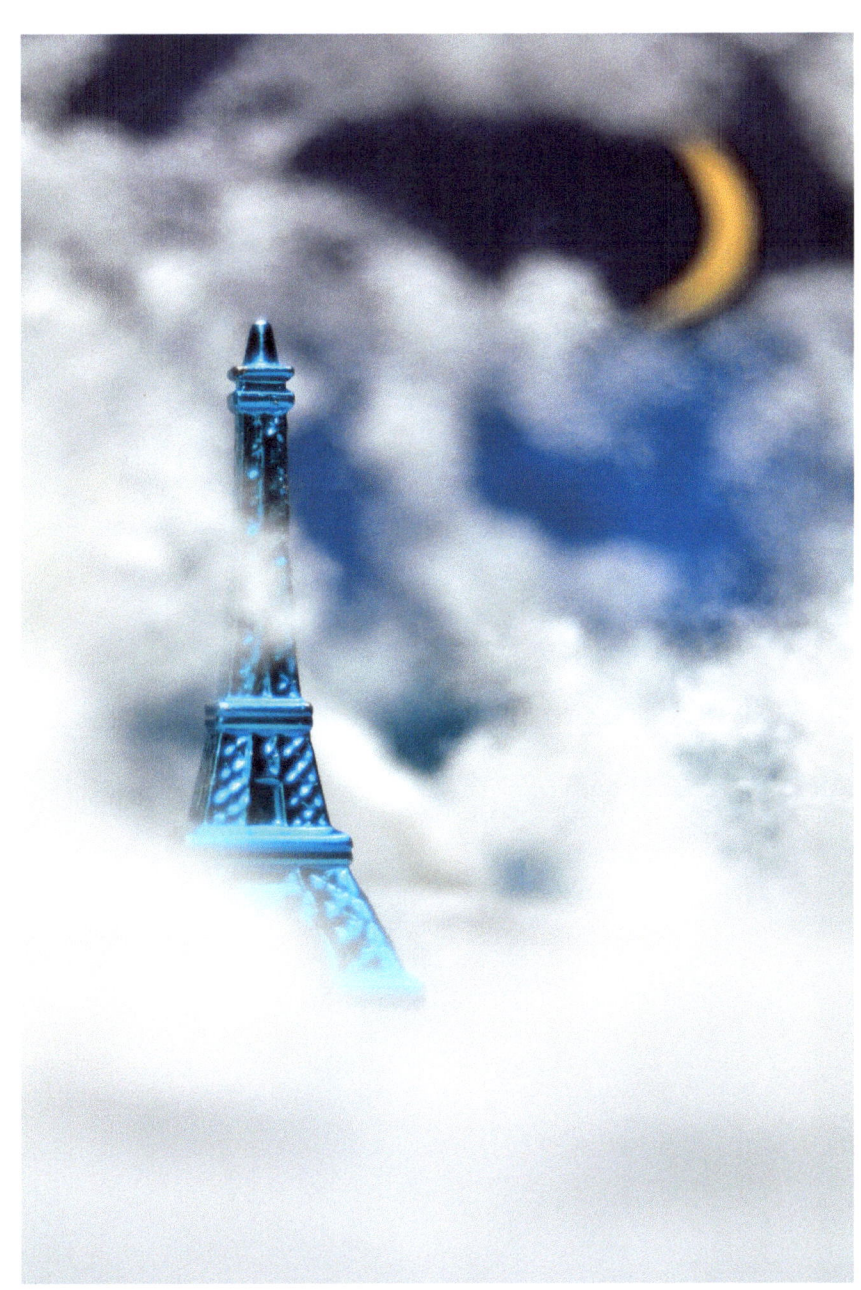

Springtime In Paris

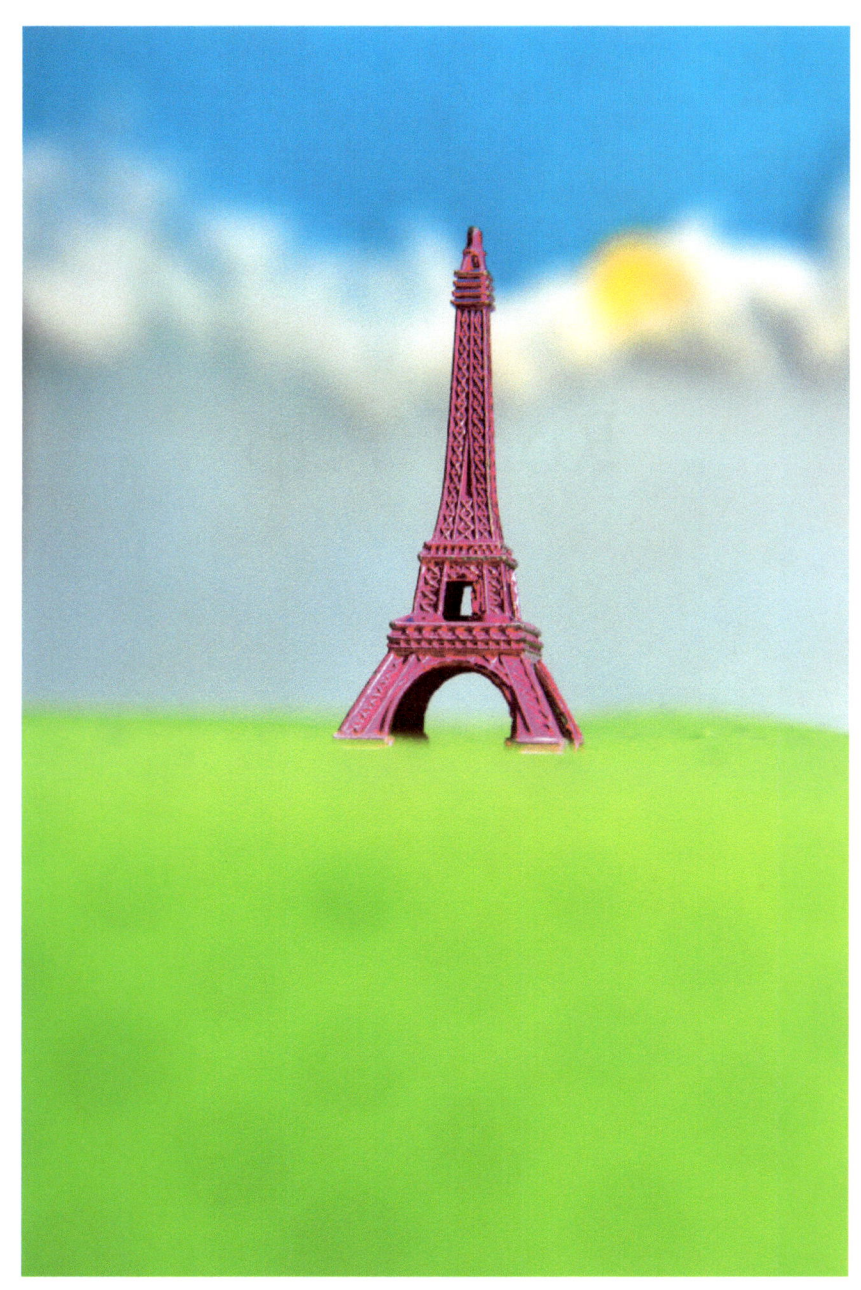

Road Trip

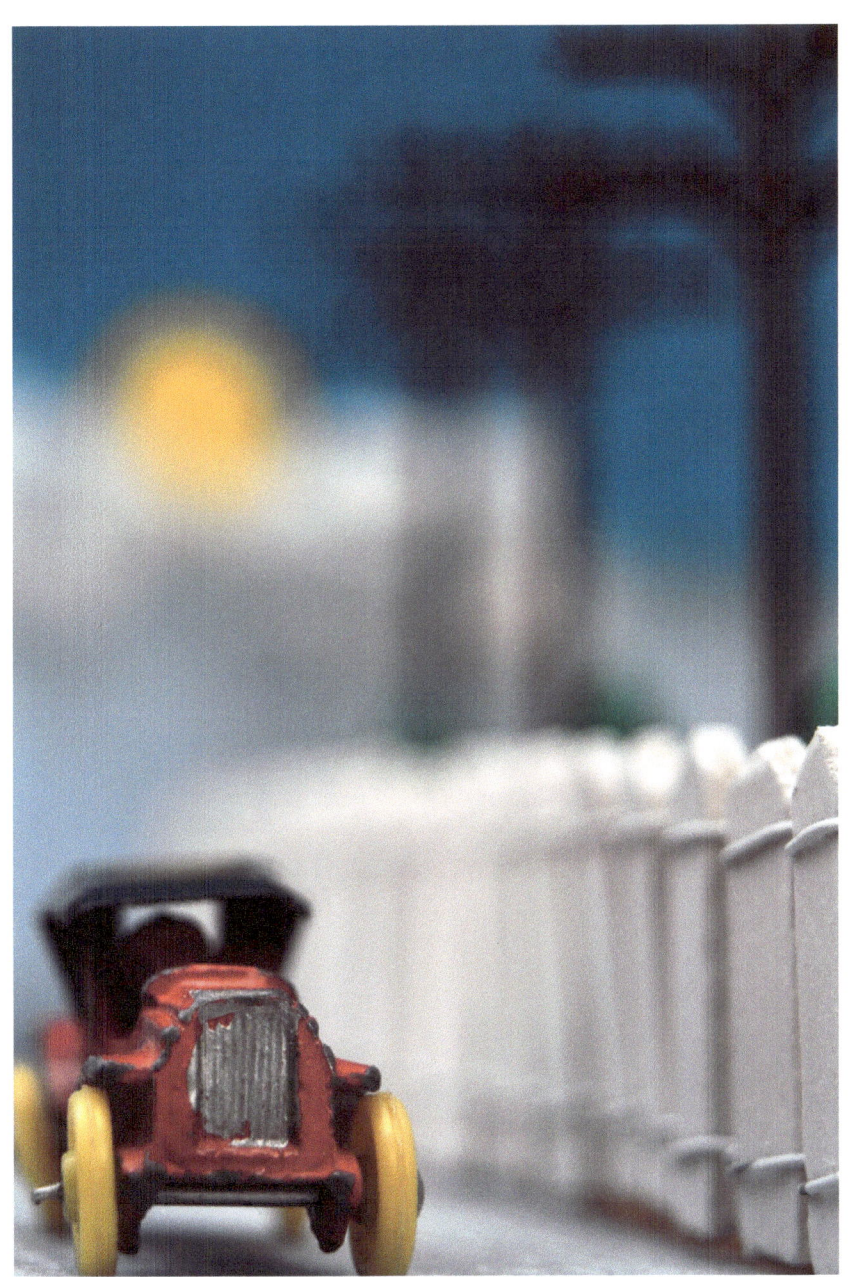

Polka Dot T

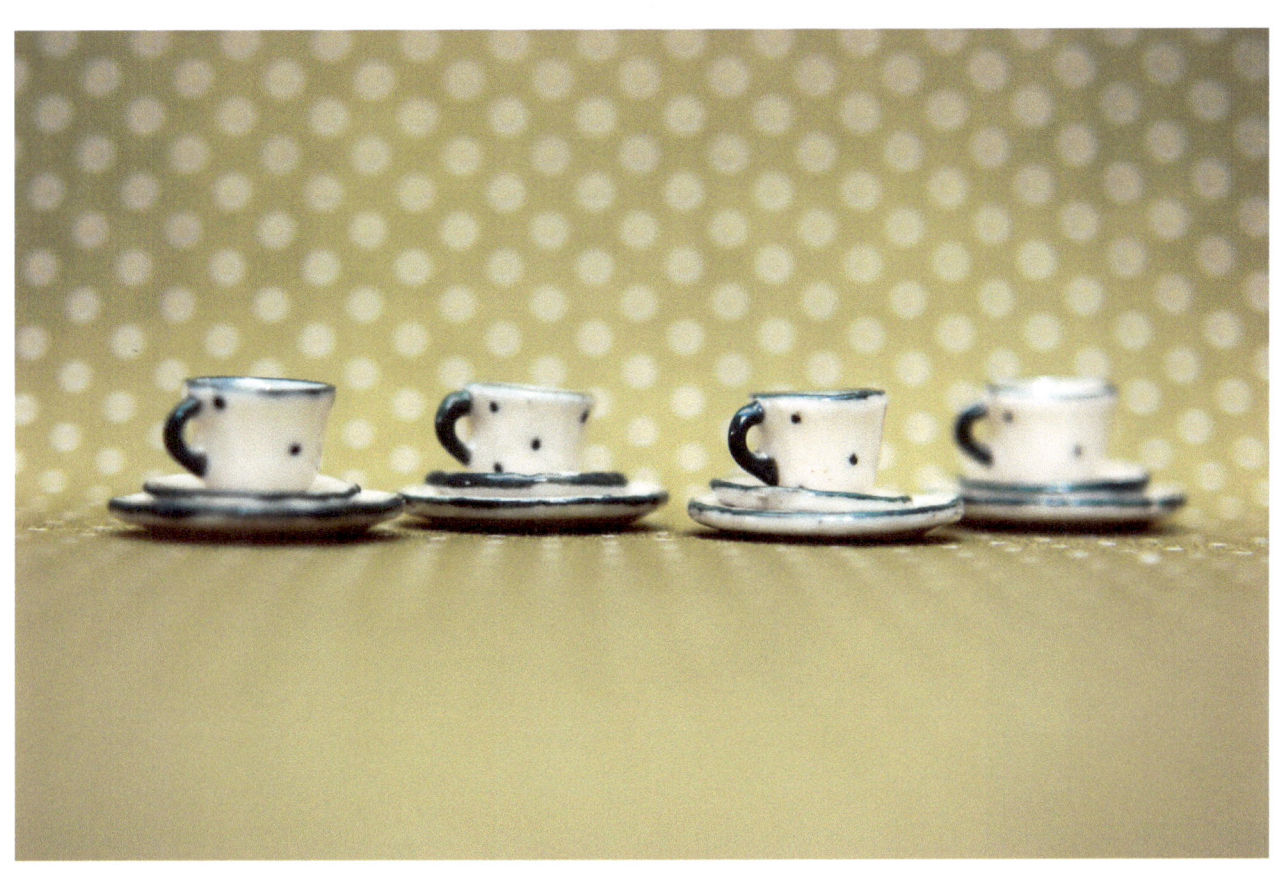

T 4 2

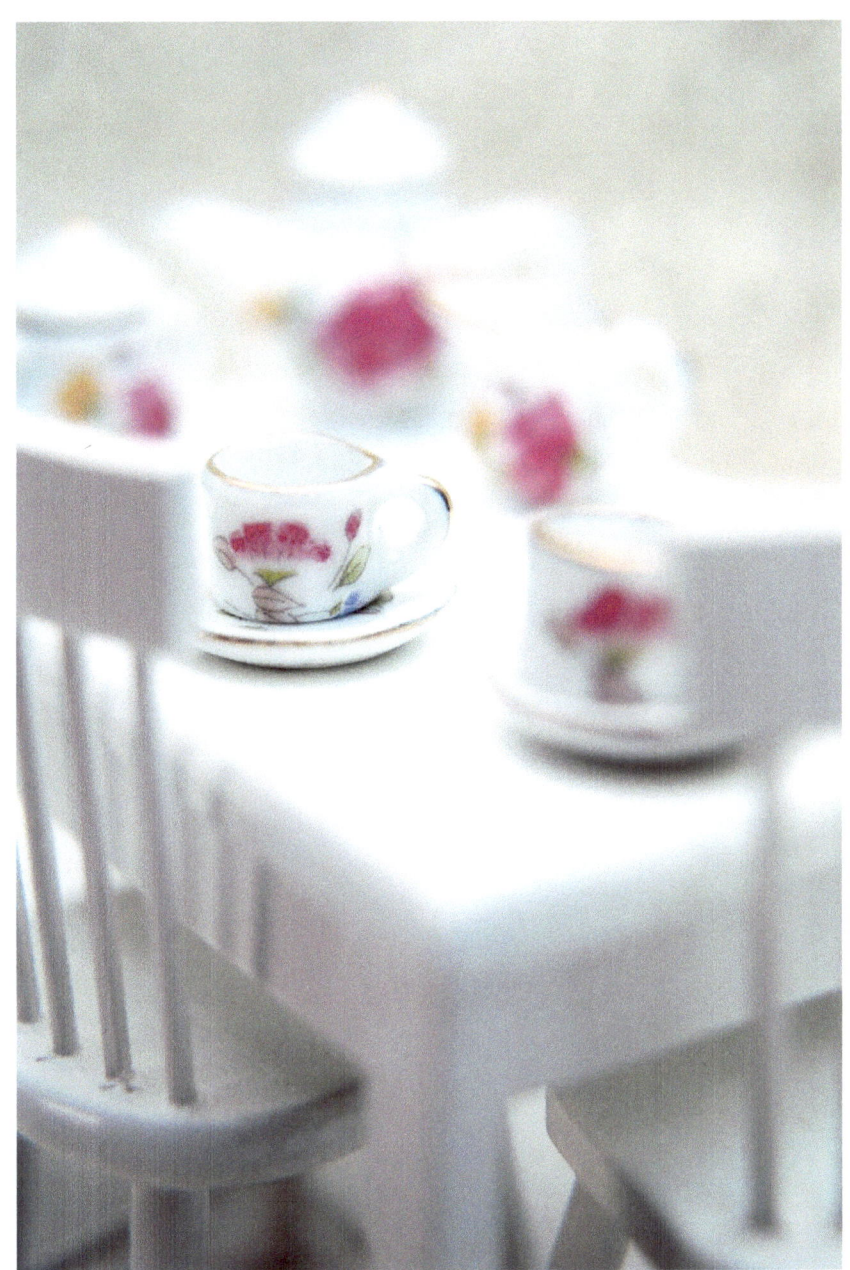

Post Klatch

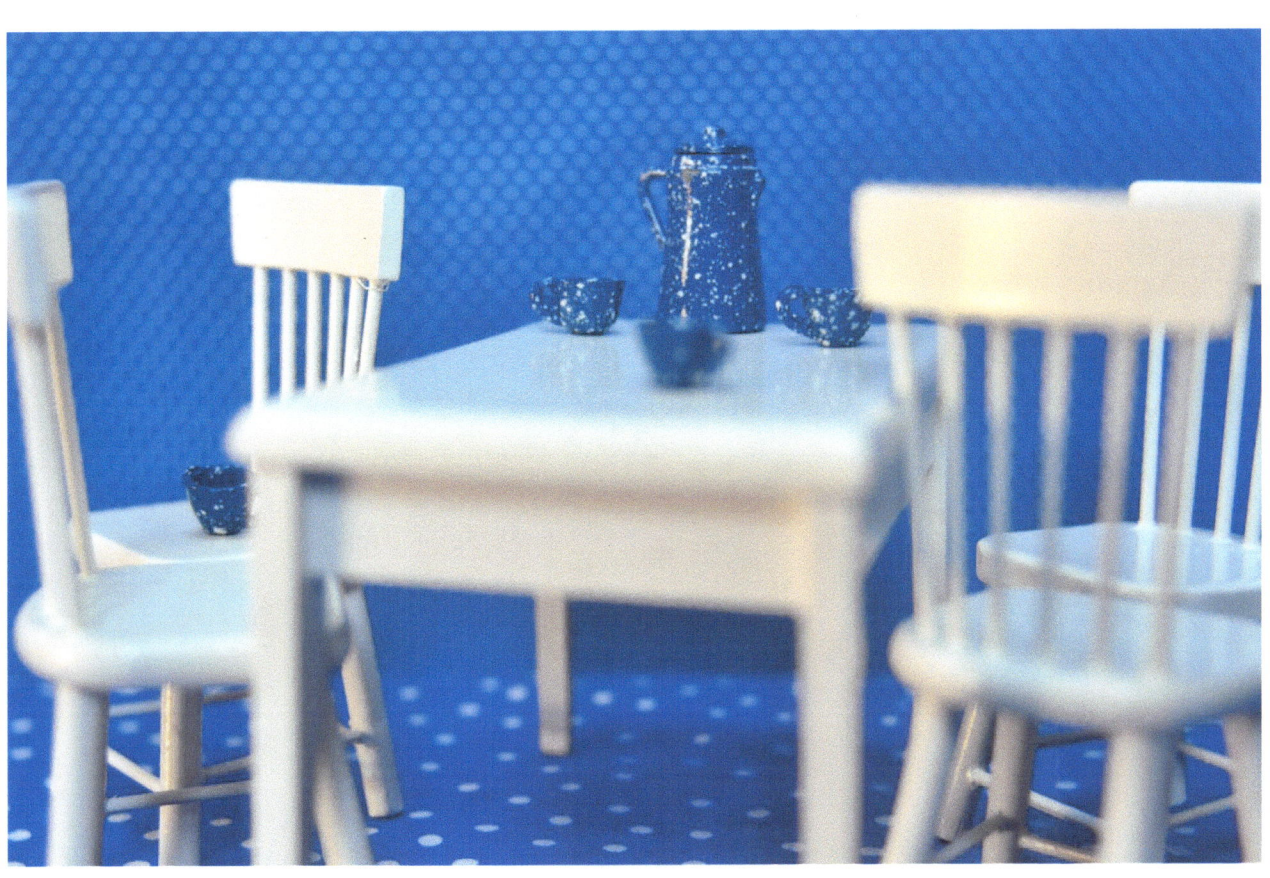

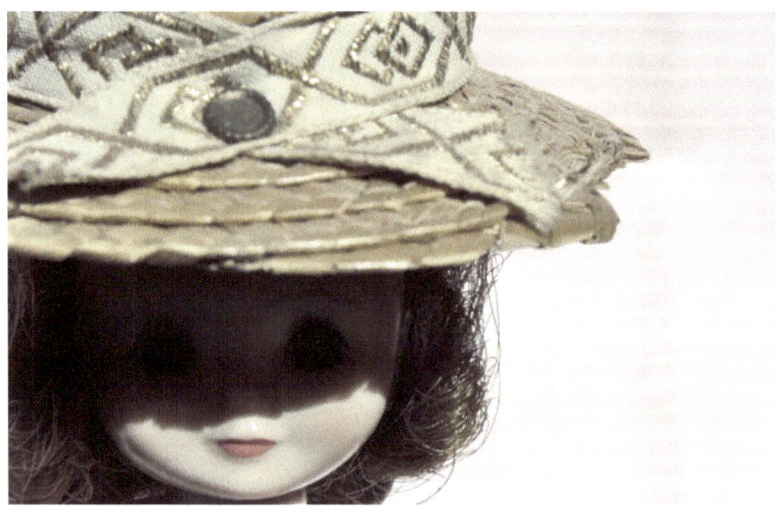

To follow this on-going project and to purchase prints of these photos go to
susancunninghamphotography.com

www.ingramcontent.com/pod-product-compliance
Lightning Source LLC
Chambersburg PA
CBHW050732180526
45159CB00003B/1196